MW01482024

ENDORSEMENTS

Practical. Transforming. Refreshing. Motivating. Helpful insights for planning a meaningful life with less stress and more peace of mind. The goals we pursue run headlong into roadblocks and sideways forces we do not control. Discover the tools to use that help you to move forward into a life of greater fulfillment and joy.

—Ken Warren, MDiv
Connections Pastor, Gateway Community Church
Washougal, Washington

Dr. Pousche has done an excellent job of capturing the nuances of the zigzags of life. His book is filled with vivid, down-to-earth life illustrations along with relevant and practical helps for when you hit your own zigs and zags. A fun and challenging read!

—Rev. Randy L. Brandt, MDiv
Chaplain, colonel US Army, retired
CBAmerica Director of Chaplaincy

What keeps us from thriving in life? We focus on difficulties like conflicts with others, health problems, demanding schedules, and overwhelming responsibilities. Our best plans and efforts are thwarted by persistent obstacles and dilemmas. Life changes direction in ways we didn't expect or want.

Life is not a straight line but a series of twist and turns. In Dr. Tom Pousche's book, The Zigzag Principle, he uses the colorful stories of his life to bring home practical applications of timeless biblical principles. His book reflects years of experience as a pastor, chaplain, and counselor while providing essential hands-on directions for our journey on life's every changing pathways.

—Dr. Bart Fowler, PsyD,
Psychologist

THE
ZIGZAG
PRINCIPLE

NAVIGATING THE TWISTS
AND TURNS OF LIFE

THE
ZIGZAG
PRINCIPLE

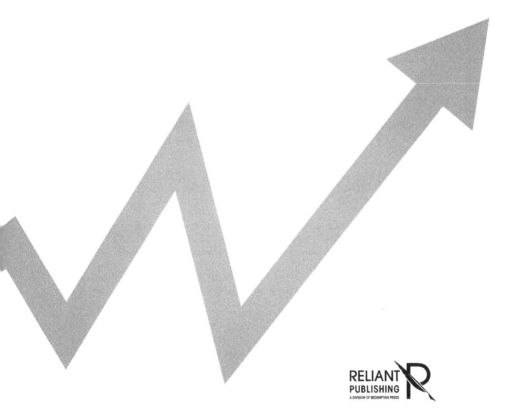

RELIANT
PUBLISHING
A DIVISION OF REDEMPTION PRESS

TOM POUSCHE

© 2021 by Tom Pousche. All rights reserved.

Published by Reliant Publishing, an imprint of Redemption Press, PO Box 427, Enumclaw, WA 98022.

Toll-Free (844) 2REDEEM (273-3336)

Redemption Press is honored to present this title in partnership with the author. The views expressed or implied in this work are those of the author. Redemption Press provides our imprint seal representing design excellence, creative content, and high-quality production.

No part of this publication may be reproduced, stored in a retrieval system, or transmitted in any way by any means—electronic, mechanical, photocopy, recording, or otherwise—without the prior permission of the copyright holder, except as provided by US copyright law.

Scriptures marked HCSB are taken from the HOLMAN CHRISTIAN STANDARD BIBLE (HCSB): Scripture taken from the HOLMAN CHRISTIAN STANDARD BIBLE, copyright© 1999, 2000, 2002, 2003 by Holman Bible Publishers, Nashville Tennessee. All rights reserved.

Scriptures marked NLT are taken from the HOLY BIBLE, NEW LIVING TRANSLATION (NLT): Scriptures taken from the HOLY BIBLE, NEW LIVING TRANSLATION, Copyright© 1996, 2004, 2007 by Tyndale House Foundation. Used by permission of Tyndale House Publishers, Inc., Carol Stream, Illinois 60188. All rights reserved. Used by permission.

Scriptures marked ISV are taken from the INTERNATIONAL STANDARD VERSION (ISV): Scripture taken from INTERNATIONAL STANDARD VERSION, copyright© 1996-2008 by the ISV Foundation. All rights reserved internationally.

Scriptures marked KJV are taken from the KING JAMES VERSION (KJV): KING JAMES VERSION, public domain.

Scriptures marked NCV are taken from the NEW CENTURY VERSION (NCV): Scripture taken from the NEW CENTURY VERSION*. Copyright© 2005 by Thomas Nelson, Inc. Used by permission. All rights reserved.

Scriptures marked NIV are taken from the NEW INTERNATIONAL VERSION (NIV): Scripture taken from THE HOLY BIBLE, NEW INTERNATIONAL VERSION *. Copyright© 1973, 1978, 1984, 2011 by Biblica, Inc.TM. Used by permission of Zondervan

Scriptures marked NKJV are taken from the NEW KING JAMES VERSION (NKJV): Scripture taken from the NEW KING JAMES VERSION*. Copyright© 1982 by Thomas Nelson, Inc. Used by permission. All rights reserved.

Scriptures marked ESV are taken from the THE HOLY BIBLE, ENGLISH STANDARD VERSION (ESV): Scriptures taken from THE HOLY BIBLE, ENGLISH STANDARD VERSION. * Copyright© 2001 by Crossway, a publishing ministry of Good News Publishers. Used by permission.

Scriptures marked TLB are taken from the THE LIVING BIBLE (TLB): Scripture taken from THE LIVING BIBLE copyright© 1971. Used by permission of Tyndale House Publishers, Inc., Carol Stream, Illinois 60188. All rights reserved.

Scriptures marked TM are taken from the THE MESSAGE: THE BIBLE IN CONTEMPORARY ENGLISH (TM): Scripture taken from THE MESSAGE: THE BIBLE IN CONTEMPORARY ENGLISH, copyright©1993, 1994, 1995, 1996, 2000, 2001, 2002. Used by permission of NavPress Publishing Group

ISBN: 978-1-64645-192-0 (Paperback)
978-1-64645-193-7 (ePub)
978-1-64645-194-4 (Mobi)

Library of Congress Catalog Card Number: 2020913971

Dedication

To Kathy, the loyal love of my life
To Scott and Anna, the son and wife I truly love
To Pam and Brett, the daughter and husband of delight

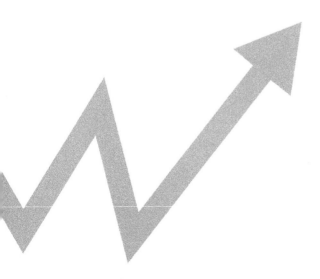

For I know the thoughts that I think toward you,
    saith the LORD,
        thoughts of peace, and not of evil,
        to give you an expected end.
            —Jeremiah 29:11 (KJV)

Trust in the LORD with all your heart
and lean not on your own understanding;
        in all your ways submit to him,
        and he will make your paths straight.
            —Proverbs 3:5–6 (NIV)

CONTENTS

Foreword   xiii

Acknowledgments   xv

Chapter 1   A Crooked Road   17

Chapter 2   Zigzag   25

Chapter 3   Zigging or Zagging   41

Chapter 4   Zigzag Challenges   53

Chapter 5   Zigzag Realities   69

Chapter 6   Zigzag Tips   83

Chapter 7   Precarious Curves   103

Chapter 8   First Things First   123

Chapter 9   Stay Focused   135

Chapter 10   A Sense of Humor   145

Chapter 11   The Big Picture   153

Chapter 12   Stay on Track   161

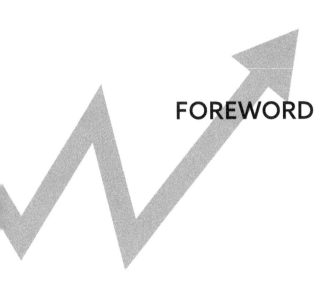

FOREWORD

I have had many students during my forty years of teaching at Western Seminary and a few disciples. Dr. Tom Pousche is one of those disciples. During my class lectures on the Bible, Tom was an attentive listener and engaged learner. But he didn't leave it at that.

Once a week Tom and I would meet together in my office where he usually came with a list of questions. After doing my best to answer Tom's questions, we would talk about his work as a transit driver, and later as a chaplain for drivers. And while we talked, Tom would tell me stories about his service in the Navy on the island of Guam, as well as his truck and bus driving experiences. Tom tells great stories. And they are stories that are not only fun to hear, but they are usually attached to a spiritual lesson.

I remember when Tom took me to lunch and Bible study at one of his favorite truck stops. After returning to my office, Tom asked, "Carl, did you notice that woman at the truck stop?" Well, I couldn't help noticing her with her platinum hair and tight-fitting clothes. I figured she was the wife of one of the truckers. "No," Tom explained, "she's a prostitute and she was walking around looking for business." I was sure naïve!

But I learned from Tom that day that not everything is as it appears. And we have to be observant and alert to the dangers lurking around us in this sin-infested and fallen world.

In this book, Dr. Tom Pousche presents, develops, and illustrates what he calls the Zigzag Principle. Tom learned this principle from Scripture and has experienced it in his own life. The stories he tells about the Zigzag Principle will help you avoid some of the mistakes Tom has made. In addition, you will have a better understanding of what is going on in your own life when you encounter a zigzag.

Tom is an enthusiastic follower of Jesus, lover of people, a published author, a seasoned teacher, and a passionate preacher. Beyond that, Tom is deeply committed to serving God's people around the world. We share a lot in common. But that shouldn't surprise me. Jesus said, "After a disciple has been fully trained, he will be like his teacher." I am thankful to God for having a small part in Tom's life and ministry. And I am proud to be his friend.

I enjoyed reading this book and was both encouraged and spiritually edified by Tom's message. I am confident that you are going to enjoy it too. And you will get to know Dr. Tom Pousche better as you read his stories and see how they illustrate and apply the zigzag principle.

J. Carl Laney
Western Seminary professor, retired

ACKNOWLEDGMENTS

S pecial thanks to:
  Kathy Pousche, my most beloved wife, mother, and best friend, a remarkable lady of marital character and integrity.

Scott, my son and his wife, Anna, who are living proof that Christian homes with Word-centered principles really work.

Pamela, my daughter and her husband, Brett, who love God, and have chosen to serve in the marketplace. You bring great joy to our family!

Iva Jean Weaver, a most beloved mother-in-law who was my best cheerleader and example, and is in heaven among the great cloud of witnesses.

Hazel Stein, a godly 103-year-old lady who faithfully supported, encouraged, and faithfully prayed for the completion of this book.

Beverly Beem, a loyal friend and first reader who has been a true friend since my Navy days at the Christian Servicemen's Center in Guam.

Gary Scott, a past fellow employee and computer specialist who has been instrumental in helping me for endless hours with all my computer needs.

Bart Fowler, a trusted colleague, friend, and fellow counselor and coffee drinker who has been an inspiration in the writing of this book.

Inger Logelin, a very special editor who is worth her weight in gold, thanks for all the hard work on my two books.

Di Tasso Coffee Shop, a coffee spot in Camas, Washington, where Dr. Bart Fowler and I worked on the psychology of my book.

PEFA, Kenya, Africa, thanks for my ministry in Kenya. I love your churches, Bible institutes, and for allowing me to write my book in Africa.

The Achar Family who provided delightful hospitality as I ministered and wrote in their home in Kisumu, Kenya, Africa. Friends forever.

Bishop Samuel of South B Church, Bless you, Bishop, for your love and support as I ministered in Nairobi, Kenya and worked out many details in this book.

CHAPTER ONE

A Crooked Road

As a truck driver, one of my greatest joys is driving down the interstates, highways and roads of America. While I take in the beauty of the scenery around me, I know to watch out when encountering curves and switchbacks. When the road ahead becomes bumpy and unpredictably crooked, I know I have to pay more attention to where I am going.

The road of life is not always a straight path forward. We are surprised by unexpected winding and crooked paths as we travel through life. Life doesn't always conform to our expectations. When the road ahead becomes bumpy and unpredictably crooked, that's when I know I need to pay attention.

I call those curves and switchbacks zigzags and recognize they help keep me focused. Merriam-Webster's Collegiate Dictionary defines a zigzag as "one of a series of short sharp turns, angles, or alterations in a course."

Let me tell you a story about a journey that taught me about zigzags—and alterations in my course.

In the fall of 2002 I was asked to be the main speaker at a three-day Village Missions church conference that was to be held in Willow Creek, California. Since the conference involved training and motivational speaking, I quickly accepted the invitation.

There was not a cloud in the sky as I left our home in Portland, Oregon on the seven-hour, 439-mile drive to Willow Creek. As I drove south on I-5, the kaleidoscope of fall colors was breathtaking.

I arrived in Willow Creek in mid-afternoon to a smell of fresh-cut lumber. The massive skyscraper trees added to the laid back country feeling. In the middle of the town square stood a gigantic wooden replica of Bigfoot.

Driving past Bigfoot, I saw the motel that had been reserved for me located next to the Willow Creek China Flat museum. After unpacking, I was so curious about this mythical creature called Bigfoot (also known as Sasquatch), that I took the time to tour the museum.

I really enjoyed meeting the town's people. They were cordial Humboldt County folk who were very accepting and polite, delightful people who loved bragging about their town, and of course, Bigfoot.

Willow Creek was a quiet, sleepy town. I found I could actually hear myself think as I stood in the town square and heard the wind moving through the tall evergreen trees.

Living on Hell Street

Back in Portland, it wasn't quiet or peaceful, but chaotic, busy, and nerve-racking. Kathy and I moved to the Northwest city shortly after we married in the summer of 1980. We found an apartment on Buchanan Avenue, one of the busiest places in the north Portland area that connected to a street called Fessenden.

What an eye-opener! We later learned that our avenue that joined with Fessenden Street was the main trucking route through the city. Some of the loudest semi-trucks came through with their

Jake brakes on, making it impossible to sleep at night.

Buchanan Avenue was a place where people congregated and stayed up all hours of the night fighting and brawling. Between the loud trucks and ornery people yelling and carrying on, it was difficult for hard working people to sleep. It was awful!

It was a happy day when Kathy and I moved about a year later to the Southeast Portland area to manage apartments. I had returned to seminary, and by managing apartments, we received free rent, which helped with our finances.

The frustrating thing was that we traded the very busy, noisy area of Buchanan Avenue in north Portland, for an unbelievable, drug-infested, obnoxious, partying street called S.E. Division Avenue.

S.E. Division was a rat race with people, cars, buses, and trucks whizzing by all day. This all took place just fifty feet from our front door. I'm still in disbelief that we managed those apartments for three and a half years. To this day I still call that street "Hell Street"!

No wonder I enjoyed my experience in Willow Creek, California. I have often said, "Either get away and come apart, or you will come apart." This speaking engagement gave me the ability to get away. As a matter of fact, instead of me being a blessing to Willow Creek, I'm convinced Willow Creek became a huge blessing to me that weekend.

The conference went extremely well. But all good things must come to an end. Even though I preached, taught, and counseled for those three days, I came away refreshed, having had the time of my life!

Mid-afternoon I checked out of my motel room and immediately went to the neighborhood gas station to fill up my tank before hitting the road. This was my last opportunity to take one last big breath and enjoy this delightful little town before heading back to the asphalt jungle of Portland.

"Take the Scenic Route"

As the attendant finished topping off my gas tank, he suggested that I consider taking the scenic way home. He pointed to the highway just in front of his gas station, and said, "It's not only a peaceful ride, but will save you a good hour or two from backtracking to I-5."

It sounded like a great idea. Besides, I was up for a little more of this peace and quiet. So I paid him and got in my car, all set to enjoy the ride home through this peaceful, scenic drive. As I took a right, heading north, and began making my journey to the Oregon border, I was anticipating a great ride filled with vistas of farm lands and animals.

However, to my surprise, about five miles out of town, the road took an unusual snakelike turn, which caused me to brake harder than normal. After getting around the curve, I reapplied the cruise control.

Without warning, there was another twisty turn, followed by another. I blurted out loud, "When will this stop?"

That's when I saw the sign "Narrow Road." I could not believe what I was reading! I wanted to go back to that gas station and give that guy a piece of my mind.

By this time, I was miles from Willow Creek and decided to keep going. After about another ten miles, I saw a sign that read "Steep Grade." I found myself climbing up a mountain with the road still snaking back and forth!

Who could enjoy the scenery while trying to navigate through all these switchbacks? I was committed after driving close to a hundred miles, so I had no choice but to follow this dizzying, narrow road.

Why did I listen to that guy? I thought. A few moments later, I said aloud what I was thinking: "Why did I come this way in the first place?"

Either way, it was way too late to be debating my mistake.

About then, I was relieved to see the road ahead was

straightening.

Does this sound like your life at times? Do you wonder how you got on the zigzag journey you are on? Does where you are in life feel like a mistake?

Let me tell you what I learned about the zigzags of life at another time of my life.

Going From Bad to Worse

Back in Bible school, I had taken a nice summer job driving semi-truck for an oil company out of Gillette, Wyoming. Driving truck is something I really enjoy, and it sure helped pay my school bills.

On one of my trips hauling oil pipe back to the trucking yard, I stopped in at a restaurant for a quick sandwich. When a guy sitting at the next table struck up a conversation with me, I learned he was a foreman on a road construction crew that was building a bridge on one of the roads just outside Gillette.

The man moved to my table and asked, "Would you be interested in working for me?"

The more he spoke about the job, the money, and the fact that they paid weekly, the more interested I became.

Before I left the restaurant that day, I had a new job! Without even giving a second thought, I immediately went and resigned my trucking job. My boss tried talking me out of it. But my mind was made up—I was quitting!

The following Monday morning, I showed up and reported in for my first day as a construction laborer. I immediately was assigned to a grouchy elderly man who had a bad attitude, smoked cigars, and loved telling dirty jokes.

By the end of the day, I was totally fed up with this perverted man who annoyed me to no end. Our jobs were tedious and repetitive. We were assigned strips of wire about ten inches long, which we would bend and twist around bigger pre-laid rebar steel that was laid the length of the bridge span. I later learned that those little wires kept the bigger rebar in place, keeping it from shifting while cement was being poured over it.

The job was a no-brainer, and I wanted out of it in the worst way. But a friend encouraged me to ride it out, saying, "Tom, you need to work on your character in holding down a job." I can't believe that I bought into this reasoning, but I toughed it out for the next eight weeks.

This was the worst job I have ever taken. To add insult to injury, word got out to all the truck drivers who knew me at the company. They would drive by the bridge site in their big rigs and blow their airhorns at me. It was terrible!

I could not wait for the day to come when I returned to Bible school. In fact, that fall semester after returning, I made my best grades ever. Perhaps there was a little truth to that character trait my friend had pointed out to me.

The bottom line is simple: I learned something from that windy road from Willow Creek, and from sticking with that terrible job. We all want a simple, straight path to follow, and want things to go our way. However, there will be curves ahead. Expect them!

Many of us want to go our own way, and make our own rules for life. But we'd do well to follow the signposts in the Bible that will help us on our journey.

King David is a great example of this principle. When his road became impossible to travel he pleaded, "Answer me when I call to you, my righteous God. Give me relief from my distress; have mercy on me and hear my prayer" (Ps. 4:1 NIV).

The Old Testament word for trust is the same word in the New Testament for the words faith and believe. It is interesting to note that the word trust occurs 152 times in the Old Testament, and gives a Hebrew rendering of words signifying "to take refuge" (Ruth 2:12); "to lean on" (Ps. 56:3); "to roll on" (Ps. 22:8); and "to wait for" (Job 35:14).

If your road happens to be crooked right now, remember you can take refuge in the Lord, lean on Him, roll your cares onto Him, and wait for Him to show you the way.

Chapter One Review
A Crooked Road

Discussion:

We all want a simple, straight path to follow, and want things to go our way, however, there will be curves ahead. Be alert for what God wants to show you in the unexpected circumstances of life.

1. What was the big deal about what I experienced when I arrived in Willow Creek?
2. Why do you think the remoteness in Willow Creek had such a personal effect on me?
3. Why is getting away and "coming apart" important? How would you explain this to a friend?
4. The gas station attendant who advised me to take the scenic road was trying to be helpful. How did taking the scenic road help or hurt?
5. Psalm 4:1 speaks of God giving relief. Can Christians really trust God to do that? Give a testimony on how God lifted a heavy load from your shoulders.

Goal Setting

What are some goals you would like to achieve?

_____

_____

_____

_____

CHAPTER TWO

Zigzag

I was sitting alone in the cafeteria of my junior high school back in the mid sixties enjoying a delicious sandwich my mom had prepared for me, when an unfamiliar student came walking by with his hot lunch tray and sat down across from me.

He appeared to be outgoing and nice as he introduced himself without reservation and said he was a sophomore. From the start, I really liked him. I can't remember his name, or what we talked about during that half hour we sat together. But the one thing I do remember—his love for math.

"I learned the most interesting principle in my geometry class this morning," he told me.

After a few moments, my curiosity got the best of me, and I asked, "What did you learn?"

Without missing a beat, his face beaming, he began telling me some enthusiastic facts about geometry. He said, "Do you know what the shortest distance between two points is?" Before I could even get a word out of my mouth he blurted out, "It's a straight line!"

I didn't realize that day that I had just heard a principle that would follow me throughout my life. I was just a kid barely passing algebra and struggling to stay in school. While I didn't fully understand its meaning, I was beginning to realize God doesn't always lead us in straight lines. I had a glimmer of hope for the struggles I was facing and the beginnings of a different perspective on the twists and turns in my life.

When You Want to Go Straight

From that day on, the reality that life was a series of zigzags not only followed me through the rest of my high school years into the Navy, and through my college years. But it wasn't until one day while I was sitting in a seminary class that this math principle came alive for me.

That morning our Old Testament professor, Dr. Stanley Ellison, was teaching the biblical account of the children of Israel in the wilderness in Exodus 13:17–22.

I listened to this dramatic scriptural account about how God used Moses to confront a wicked and power-hungry king, and ask him to let God's people go.

That really caught my attention. The first thing that popped into my mind was, Right, like this king was just going to roll over and play dead. He wasn't just going to sign a release order to allow people who worked for him—who were his slaves—to waltz their way out of his slave camp without a problem. Chuckling to myself, I simply could not see this happening.

The funny part about the whole story is that this sadistic king would turn out to be eager to let them leave after God sent plagues to convince him.

The account of these "refugees" trying to flee Egypt and make their way to a land of milk and honey under the leadership of Moses kept me fascinated. I thought, there's nothing straight about this story. The whole story was filled with twists and turns—a series of zigzags—involving millions of people crossing a hot desert.

As the story continues, so does the drama.

They wanted to go straight to the land of Canaan. God, however, knew this was not safe.

What's so interesting about the journey to Canaan is that it should have been an easy trip. If you look on a map of the times (like the ones found in the back of your Bibles), this was a no-brainer. On the map it appears to be an easy straight-line approach, "as the crow flies," to Canaan.

Remember, these tired and worn-out people had been in captivity for hundreds of years, and all they wanted was to escape slavery and make it to the Promised Land.

Maps can sometimes be hard to read and may not give us the true picture. Routes that look straightforward on paper may actually be crooked and more complex on the road. Now keep in mind, the Israelites didn't even have maps, just knowledge of trade routes.

According to some biblical scholars, this particular straight-line approach should only have amounted to a quick five-to-seven-day road trip under the best of circumstances. If there were any surprises along the way, like road conditions or detours, the journey may have been delayed an extra week, or longer.

But the people didn't know their pathway ahead was not really a passable one. This road ahead was infested with some evil people—criminals, robbers, and rapists who would do them harm—even kill them.

Besides, God sovereignly had other plans—another zigzag. Notice what the text says: "When Pharaoh let the people go, God did not lead them by way of the land of the Philistines, although that was near. For God said, 'Lest the people change their minds when they see war and return to Egypt'" (Ex. 13:17 ESV).

God knew these Israelites were not up to a fight. Since God

knows everything, He was aware they would have retreated back to familiar territory in Egypt, if they encountered any kind of trouble.

Therefore God did not allow them to take the express route through the land of the Philistines.

Wasted Miles

This old saying is sometimes true: "The faster I go, the behinder I get!"

I had to learn that principle the hard way.

Back in the mid-70s, I was making a quick trucking trip to the Northwest, heading north on I-5 out of Los Angeles to Oregon. As I checked my instruments, I could see I was low on fuel, and planned to stop a couple of hundred miles north at a truck stop on SR 99 in Fresno, California.

As I approached an upcoming junction that separated I-5 northbound from State Route 99, which runs parallel, I got distracted and missed the exit, putting me on I-5—the wrong highway.

In this part of the state, I-5 involves driving through miles of desert with only a few places to fuel up. Whereas, Highway 99 provided several places to stop and fuel and allowed a driver to get something to eat. But I desperately needed to fuel up at the truck stop located in Fresno on SR 99.

So, instead of trying to turn myself around, I reasoned, I'll take a shortcut. I would head east across the desert, which would put me back on SR 99 northbound in no time at all. My idea was simple, and I thought it would save time, fuel, and mileage, and prevent me from having to turn around and backtrack to the interchange.

I pulled into the first rest stop, and took a quick peek at my map to make sure my idea was safe and sound. Sure enough, there was an exit about ten miles ahead, and roughly a fifty-mile run east to reconnect to SR 99. I was totally thrilled with my idea!

Unfortunately, my problem was far from over. As I approached the turnoff leaving I-5 and headed eastward on the narrow highway, it occurred to me that there were no road markings of any kind on the road I had taken.

I had a sickening feeling in my stomach. Things just didn't look right. My gut feeling told me to turn around—while my watch, and my nerves were telling me to keep going. I thought, I've come too far to turn around now. I just kept going eastward and tried not to give it a second thought.

Not more than twenty miles into this shortcut, I saw a yellow diamond-shaped sign with big black letters that read: "Low Bridge Ahead." The sign said the bridge was 12 feet, 6 inches high.

My heart sank with disappointment—my trailer was 13 feet, 6 inches high. Obviously, I could not cross the bridge since my truck was higher than the steel beams at the top of the bridge span.

This was definitely one of those "gotcha" moments. I had to slowly and creatively get the truck and trailer turned around. Then I had to backtrack a wasted fifty miles back to the junction, which put me behind schedule and wasted my fuel.

I had left God out of the picture in my plan to take that highway shortcut. The problem was not God, it was me. I was so obsessed in taking a shortcut, and afraid of running out of diesel, that I became stuck in my mindset, and had lost the ability to think straight.

God Had a Plan

Meanwhile, back to the Israelites crossing a scorching desert. What was going on there? This was a no-brainer. All it should have involved was a quick hike across a hot desert—heading on a straight path. We're talking simple stuff here! It all boiled down to several days of walking on an old trade route (a shortcut) that led directly in a straight line into the land of Canaan. It seemed to be the perfect route with no surprises—no twists or turns.

Why wouldn't almighty God allow this disorganized mob of four million people go on this straightforward northeasterly route? He wasn't directionally challenged!

What was God thinking? Didn't Yahweh have Moses' best interests in mind, as well as His people who He magnificently delivered from Egypt?

The answer is an absolute "Yes!"

How do we know that? Judges 6:8b (KJV) affirms: "That the LORD sent a prophet unto the children of Israel, which said unto them, Thus saith the LORD God of Israel, I brought you up from Egypt, and brought you forth out of the house of bondage."

This Old Testament verse assures us that God personally sent His prophet Moses to give hope and direction to a people who had been delivered out of bondage. In all the zigzags of God's sovereign leading, He had their backs covered the entire time.

He had a plan.

He knew what He was doing.

The Israelites didn't know that taking this shortcut was not only a bad idea, but it was a suicide route. Going that particular route, would most likely have cost many of them their lives. They would most likely have fallen into the hands of the worst thieves, robbers, and killers who were hanging out along this trail waiting for a golden opportunity to do harm to the Israelites.

Exodus 13:18 (ESV) clearly reads, "But God led the people around by the way of the wilderness toward the Red Sea. And the people of Israel went up out of the land of Egypt equipped for battle."

God was doing His part to protect His people. But, instead of being thankful, they chose to complain, gripe, and to find fault with the One who had just released them from a death sentence. They were simply an ungrateful people!

Here's the bottom line: God knew what was best for His people. This particular zigzag turned out to be a blessing in disguise. God saved the Israelites a lot of heartache and pain by not allowing them to go in the direction they foolishly wanted to take.

I'll say it again. This so-called shortcut that the Israelites wanted to take was nothing more than a trap filled with unscrupulous robbers and killers—evil men preying on the innocent. Once again, God had a plan—and it did not include going in the shortest direction.

God also knows what is best for you and me.

A Dumb Mistake

Back in the mid-seventies, I graduated from Bible school in Montana. A couple of my Bible school friends then decided after graduating to transfer their credit hours to a Christian liberal arts college down south in Tennessee, in the Bible Belt. They thought they could take a shortcut and save time and money in obtaining their BA degrees.

Well, I decided to follow them.

The night we graduated, the president of the Bible college specifically asked me to stick around for another year, saying I could quickly receive my BA degree there and then head off to seminary. He knew I really wanted to go on to seminary more than anything else.

But I figured heading south with my two friends and enrolling in this dream college would pay off big time for me.

Surprise! Things didn't really go the way I anticipated. What I thought would be a straight-line approach actually turned into one zigzag after the other for me.

The trouble began as I got settled into my new dorm room, and another series of zigzags popped up from out of nowhere. I became sick, which led to my grades suffering. I was frustrated as the dean of students and I didn't see eye-to-eye with each other. It was one thing after another—and it was wearing me out.

Long story short—I toughed out the first year of that college. By the time I returned to finish out my last year, everything hit the fan—resulting in my premature withdrawal from that college. I was so disappointed in the whole experience.

I regretted following my two friends south to attend that college. My best friend from Bible college ran into his own set of problems. He ended up marrying my roommate's fiancé, which was short lived. Our third friend graduated and fell off the radar screen.

Here's the point: I simply made a big dumb mistake in not listening to the president of my Bible school. That mistake cost me just under $10,000—a dreadful amount of money in the mid-70s. It also cost me two years out of my life. It was awful!

But I learned a valuable lesson through all of this zigzagging.

I learned that straight lines do not always work in real life.

A does not always lead to B.

God sometimes sovereignly permits those dreaded zigzags to exist. He gives us an opportunity to slow down as we allow Him to redirect the paths we are taking in life—much like He did for the Israelites in the wilderness.

My advice is: Don't be too quick to run from your zigzags. God just may have a valuable lesson for you.

How can I say that?

The answer is simple: God is sovereignly in control—even in chaotic circumstances. He has beneficial plans for His children who know Him as Savior. Our lives have been mapped out.

Listen to the words of Jeremiah, when he wrote these words back in the seventh century BC: "Before I formed you in the womb I knew you, and before you were born I consecrated you; I appointed you a prophet to the nations" (Jer. 1:5 ESV).

Another verse gives an added perspective. "I know what I'm doing. I have it all planned out—plans to take care of you, not abandon you, plans to give you the future you hope for" (Jer. 29:11 MSG).

Another Old Testament king, King Solomon, known as the wisest man in the Old Testament, penned words that have echoed down through history. He wrote: "Trust God from the bottom of your heart; don't try to figure out everything on your own. Listen for God's voice in everything you do, everywhere you go; he's the one who will keep you on track" (Prov. 3:5–6 MSG).

Stuck in a "Slave Mentality"

No matter what God or Moses did or didn't do to make the restless wanderers comfortable—they were still suffering from an illness better known as "a slave mentality." There were no magic pills available for the kind of mindset they were exhibiting.

The Bible is clear, zigzags are a good thing! They are intended not to do anyone harm, but to serve as a cushion of hope and direction in keeping the people of God on the right paths in life. Read the following text and see God's hand of protection and love for His people:

> Then the Lord said to Moses, "Tell the people of Israel to turn back and encamp in front of Pi-hahiroth, between Migdol and the sea, in front of Baal-zephon; you shall encamp facing it, by the sea. For Pharaoh will say of the people of Israel, 'They are wandering in the land; the wilderness has shut them in.' And I will harden Pharaoh's heart, and he will pursue them, and I will get glory over Pharaoh and all his host, and the Egyptians shall know that I am the Lord." And they did so.
>
> When the king of Egypt was told that the people had fled, the mind of Pharaoh and his servants was changed toward the people, and they said, "What is this we have done, that we have let Israel go from serving

us?" So he made ready his chariot and took his army with him, and took six hundred chosen chariots and all the other chariots of Egypt with officers over all of them. And the Lord hardened the heart of Pharaoh king of Egypt, and he pursued the people of Israel while the people of Israel were going out defiantly. The Egyptians pursued them, all Pharaoh's horses and chariots and his horsemen and his army, and overtook them encamped at the sea, by Pi-hahiroth, in front of Baal-zephon.

When Pharaoh drew near, the people of Israel lifted up their eyes, and behold, the Egyptians were marching after them, and they feared greatly. And the people of Israel cried out to the Lord. They said to Moses, "Is it because there are no graves in Egypt that you have taken us away to die in the wilderness? What have you done to us in bringing us out of Egypt? Is not this what we said to you in Egypt: 'Leave us alone that we may serve the Egyptians'? For it would have been better for us to serve the Egyptians than to die in the wilderness." And Moses said to the people, "Fear not, stand firm, and see the salvation of the Lord, which he will work for you today. For the Egyptians whom you see today, you shall never see again." (Ex. 14:1–13 ESV)

We are no different than the people of Israel. We too complain and gripe when things don't go our way. We too head off into wrong directions and unknown paths in our lives here on Planet Earth.

It appears that these Israelites were like prisoners of war (POWs) who had developed a slave mentality in the slave camps of Egypt. They were confused and just plain exhausted.

But the Scriptures echo God's mercy when dealing with them. He knew just how tired and miserable they had become. Exodus 13:17–18 (MSG) says: "'If the people encounter war, they'll change their minds and go back to Egypt.' So God led the people on the wilderness road, looping around to the Red Sea."

This passage tells us God knew how much pain the Israelites had been through. He also knew that what they could handle, and that being delivered was a major transition for them.

But these POWs were so stuck on their problems and hardships they forgot it was almighty God who delivered them. You'd think they would have been just a little grateful to God for sending Moses to deliver them.

On the contrary, due to their slave mentality—they had become victims long before Moses showed up. Choosing to be stuck in their circumstances, they were not happy campers. To them, the Almighty could do nothing right!

But these were a people precious to God, that He loved. His intentions for them were good—very good!

As we follow their wilderness story, it becomes clear God purposely led them on what I would call a zigzag path.

Why in the world would a loving, sovereign, all-knowing God do that?

I believe God wanted to keep them in His captivity.

There is also another good reason for God to lead them in a zigzag manner. He was protecting them from the evil that would do them in if they were allowed to take that straight-line approach in making their way Canaan.

There were three possible routes they could have taken.

The first route to Canaan involved going northeast (a straight line). But the Israelites forgot God and left Him out of their planning. Perhaps they forgot God is omnipresent—He's everywhere. No one can elude Him or hide from His presence.

Bible scholars suggest that allowing the people of Israel to take the easy route would ultimately have led to danger. The easy route was an invasion route, fortified with enemy garrisons hiding along the way. It would have involved them in big battles for which they were not prepared.

The second possible route involved going a little south, then heading east across the Negev (Beersheba). God, in His sovereignty, did not permit them to go that way either.

The Israelites did not take into account that God is omnipotent—all powerful. He's able to straighten out what is crooked. He raises up kings and takes them down. He is supremely sovereign and powerful. He's in total, complete, unequivocal control, and only gives His very best to His precious children.

The third route involved the Israelites heading further south—going around modern Mai-lean (or Milian). This route would eventually and safely lead to the Promised Land without any surprises.

By leading them on this route, God proved He had His peoples' good in mind.

God knows what's best for His children whom He is leading along life's precarious pathways.

In this wilderness story we see God was patient and compassionate with this testy crowd of people. Like wonderful, godly parents who love and want the best for their children, almighty God wanted the very best for these wandering Israelites. While they were sometimes unconvinced that His intentions were good, and that He would safely lead them to the Promised Land.

That day in seminary when we studied the wilderness story of the children of Israel, I was so impressed that I literally ran home and developed a sermon on Exodus 13. Here's my original homiletical outline I created that afternoon.

Text: Exodus 13:17–22

Title: The Zigzagging of God's Will

Subject: Signposts ahead

Theme: God's sovereignty in leading His people along

Aim: To teach on God's competence to protect, lead, and guide

Proposition: God is Here to Get You There

Interrogative: How can I rest assured that God is here to get me there?

Propositional Transition: Believers can rest assured of God's sovereign leading by understanding two simple facts from Exodus 13:17–22.

Outline:
1. God Has a Sovereign Plan   Ex. 13:17–20
2. God Has Sovereign Means   Ex. 13: 21–22

Sometimes I pull out this homiletical outline as a reminder of God's sovereign love and faithfulness in leading His children along life's precarious zigzags (pathways) in life.

This biblical story is just as relevant for us today. Over the years, I have thanked God for His continuous love and protection in all my zigzagging moments.

As I've committed my circumstances to Him, they have worked well for me. I'm confident they will also work well for you regardless of your circumstances.

Remember, God's sovereign zigzags are not meant to harm you. They exist as evidence of God's good intentions in keeping believers on an accurate course and get them through the rough moments in life.

I'm convinced that is why Moses carried the bones of Joseph with him through the wilderness journey (Ex. 13:19). It was a reminder of God's loyal love and His good intentions as they made their way to the Promised Land.

Today God assures us that His intentions for us are still good—and active and alive today.

He extends His invitation to us to follow and trust His will for our lives in Jeremiah 33:3 (MSG): "Call to me and I will answer you. I'll tell you marvelous and wondrous things that you could never figure out on your own."

Remember, there are no straight lines in real life. Don't be too impetuous in trying to squirm out of the zigzags. They exist for your benefit. God sovereignly uses them to purposefully slow you down, giving you grace and opportunity to refocus your sights on Him.

Chapter Two Review
Zigzag

Discussion:

Learning a simple math principle about the shortest distance between two lines made a big impact on my life. But God has good intentions in allowing us to go through zigzags, as He did with the Israelites in the wilderness.

1. Give the big picture to the math principle of the shortest distance between two lines.
2. How would you explain this principle to a friend?
3. How does God use zigzags in our lives to keep us from harm or direct us?
4. What in the wilderness story of Exodus 13 especially connects with you?
5. Please share a zigzag you are presently dealing with today or have dealt with.
6. What are some lessons you've learned from zigzags?

Goal Setting

What are some goals you would like to achieve as you have read chapter two?

_____

_____

_____

_____

CHAPTER THREE

Zigging or Zagging

I was one of those students who hated junior high school. Dragging myself out of bed every morning to catch the school bus was a chore for me. One of the things that kept me attending—along with parents, and the principal, and being able to hang around lots of other kids my age—was playing dodgeball at the school gym.

I purposely arrived at school an hour early each morning just to play the game. The idea of this particular game was to stand against the gym wall facing six eager guys who stood at the red line about twenty-five feet away, staring me down. Each one was armed with three hand-sized red rubber balls and looked really eager to plaster me, thereby taking me out of the game.

As I stood there (usually with two or three other guys next to me), the intense body language of the guys opposite was filled with anticipation. When the whistle blew they commenced firing. The object was to make contact and take out as many of the players from the game as they could.

I was pretty good at dodging most of those missiles aimed at me. But every now and then someone would take a lucky shot and nail my hide to the wall with one of their supersonic balls. Fortunately, the hand-sized red rubber balls were harmless. But when they made contact, it had a brief stinging effect which usually left a small red mark. No one ever got hurt, and all of us simply loved the game. It kept us fresh, alert, and with the program.

After I had graduated from high school, and entered the United States Navy, it didn't take long for me to realize that the military was much like that dodgeball game in junior high school.

In the Navy there were all kinds of obstacles and distractions, much like those red fast balls that were hurled my direction, wanting to take me out of the game. The only difference between gym and the Navy I enlisted in, was the size and hardness of those fast-moving balls being hurled at me. In fact, as time went on, those rubber balls became bigger and faster, and left a longer stinging effect.

The Case of the Missing Seabag

One of the first fast balls came my direction when I graduated from boot camp in San Diego, California. Dressed in my "navy blues," I boarded a Navy bus which transported us to LAX International Airport in Los Angeles, from where we would fly home for a two-week leave.

At the airport, I stepped up to the ticket counter and gave my airline expense voucher to an attractive young ticket agent. By her big smile, it was obvious that my uniform impressed her.

With her eyes glued on me, she somehow lost her concentration and placed my seabag on the wrong conveyor belt—sending it the opposite direction through two big rubber doors, to the back baggage department where it would be placed on a baggage car, then placed on the wrong airline, going the wrong direction.

Not more than a moment later, she realized her mistake and assured me my bag would be located and automatically be returned to my hometown airport. Anxious to go home, I grabbed my boarding pass and left to catch my plane.

Eventually, the airlines did recover my lost seabag. By the time it arrived in Idaho Falls, Idaho, I had already left for my first duty station in Agana, Guam. It wasn't more than a couple weeks later that I received a letter from my dad saying he had picked up my seabag from the airport, and had placed it on Western Airlines to be flown to San Francisco. From there it would be placed on an overseas flight, then delivered at the post office in Guam.

At that moment, it was as if that first red dodgeball was closing in on me fast!

Every day for the next several weeks, I went to the Naval post office looking for that seabag. Again, no sea bag. To this day, I have never seen my green canvas Navy duffle bag again. It is simply lost!

A couple of years later, I stopped in at Treasure Island, near San Francisco, where all Navy lost articles are collected and stored in a gigantic building, waiting for some lucky sailor to come and retrieve his lost articles. Again, no seabag!

Losing that seabag not only caused me unnecessary frustration, but cost a ton of money—money I simply didn't have. Eventually I had to replace everything—Navy uniforms, boots, and other expensive military articles needed for active military duty. I even had to replace my new Bible that my church in Idaho Falls had given me before leaving for boot camp.

As time went on, it dawned on me that those nasty, red rubber balls aimed at me were nothing more than what I called zigzags. In other words, they were a chaotic moment attempting to bring violent disorder and mayhem into my life.

The amazing thing about zigzags is that there is no way to prepare for them. There are no bells—no whistles—no warnings of any kind. Nothing! Zilch! In fact, it's difficult to hide from them. Trying to outrun them is not an option. They just seem to randomly pop up, and usually at the wrong times in life.

These uncertain twists and turns become a nuisance, and they can easily wear people out.

They exist. They just are!

Personally, it's not the zigging that gets my goat. It's normally the zagging that does it—you know, those unpredictable, unannounced moments that somehow produce grief.

The words the apostle Paul shared with the Corinthian church during some of their zigzag experiences are assuring. He encouraged them to: "Remain alert. Keep standing firm in your faith. Keep on being courageous and strong" (1 Cor. 16:13 ISV).

Stay Focused

Those stinging red balls are only reminders to keep ourselves focused.

You still have an opportunity to turn things around. It can be done. All it takes is a little heart and a willing spirit to recognize you missed your mark. Quit throwing big rocks at yourself and get moving forward.

There was a man who lived during the Old Testament times who had a lot of experience with these kind of attacks. His name was King David. Listen to his words:

> Blessed is the man that walketh not in the counsel of the ungodly, nor standeth in the way of sinners, nor sitteth in the seat of the scornful.
>
> But his delight is in the law of the Lord; and in his law doth he meditate day and night.
>
> And he shall be like a tree planted by the rivers of water, that bringeth forth his fruit in his season; his leaf also shall not wither; and whatsoever he doeth shall prosper.
>
> The ungodly are not so: but are like the chaff which the wind driveth away.

> Therefore the ungodly shall not stand in the judgment, nor sinners in the congregation of the righteous.
>
> For the Lord knoweth the way of the righteous: but the way of the ungodly shall perish. (Ps. 1:1–6 KJV)

This profound passage of Scripture simply points to the truth that there will be zigzagging moments in life. They're just par for the course. In David's life, as well in yours and mine, red rubber balls will not go away. Expect them. Be prepared for them.

In the presidential race in 2016 there were plenty of red rubber balls hurled at Donald Trump and Hillary Clinton in their bids to be president.

Donald Trump was caught on a hot mic saying some ugly, despicable things about women. Someone with an electronic device captured his words, even though he was speaking to someone privately on a bus. That tape surfaced mysteriously some eleven years afterwards and was used in an attempt to destroy his credibility.

Not more than a week later, Hillary Clinton had a zagging moment when WikiLeaks released some damaging emails that put a spin on her secret deals with some unscrupulous people in high places overseas.

Those red rubber balls are designed to whiz through the air and take out standing targets. When you get hit with one it sure capturer your attention.

But all you have to do is to keep pedaling. It's like riding a bicycle, just keep your head high, stay focused, and enjoy the ride.

> No test or temptation that comes your way is beyond the course of what others have had to face. All you need to remember is that God will never let you down; he'll never let you be pushed past your limit; he'll always be there to help you come through it. (1 Cor. 10:13 MSG)

An Unhappy Man

It's easy to get caught up in a vicious cycle of unpredictable circumstances. You know those out-of-control moments where you feel like you are zagging when you want to be zigging. On other days you're zigging when you think you should be zagging. Either way, it is like you are spinning your wheels in the sand—going nowhere.

I often hear the word survivor used to describe these kinds of people. It typically involves those that find themselves stuck in the ruts of life, and who are not unhappy, and always blaming others for their problems.

Years ago, I was invited to a dinner party where I watched in disbelief as a disgruntled man in his nineties insulted a young man who was seated opposite him at our table. His maligning comment, after the young man complimented our hostess for the sumptuous dinner, was totally inappropriate and out of line. Without warning, this elderly man simply flipped out with harsh innuendos and insults. No sooner had his toxic explosion of words ended, this dissatisfied grouch rudely stood up and stormed away from the dinner table without a gesture of thanks to our hostess.

The hostess apologized for the man's juvenile behavior. The rude man was her father. She later spoke of her dad being a loving Christian man while she was growing up. Then came the day when he was promoted in his work with the railroad.

His new position as an inspector gave him the authority to scrutinize all the steam locomotives coming into the terminal in Chicago. He was to walk around each steam locomotive and locate potential problems that could cause breakdowns out on the line, saving the train company money and time.

After giving forty years of dedicated service to implement the company policies and putting up with irritable train engineers trying to keep their schedules, he retired and turned into a gruff gray-haired curmudgeon.

There's a German word that describes this kind of cantankerous behavior. It's the term schadenfreude, which may be translated: "The joy of destroying the joy of others." Merriam-Webster's Collegiate Dictionary defines it as "enjoyment obtained from the troubles of others."

I define it as when someone messes with someone else's joy.

A couple of guys in a joyous mood were laughing at a comment while at church. A person with a big blue armband with the word Security written on it approached them and ordered them, "Stop your joking around."

The man doing the laughing was caught off guard but returned a smile.

That is when the cranky security man informed him, "You have yellow teeth."

Suffice it to say, the church member was appalled with this wannabe policeman's schadenfreude and the church lost a member that day.

Cynical people seem to make it their mission to dampen the spirits of others who are more positive. Many of them are stressed or burned out; some may be on anti-depressants. They're the ones who are always worn out—pooped—with no adrenaline. Or they may be the successful ones who are always doing the wrong things that get them into trouble.

Making the Wrong Moves

Back in the mid-seventies, I graduated from Montana Institute of the Bible (MIB) in Billings, Montana. It was small with about sixty-plus young people who came to study the Bible and to learn more about God.

The school was going through some struggles with water, as city water had not made its way seven miles west of the city where it was located. So the college began hauling water to the campus at a cost of $500 a truck load.

Eventually, the board voted to move the campus from Billings to a very rural area they had discovered in central Montana. The new location was an abandoned Air Force radar base in a remote area called Maiden Valley—twenty-one miles out of Lewistown, Montana.

The board was all in agreement that this was a perfect solution to the ongoing water problem they were tired of fighting. So, without hesitation, they made the purchase, and moved the Bible school to their new campus in central Montana, renaming it Big Sky Bible College (BSBC).

A few years later, the city of Billings laid the waterline all the way out past the old campus of MIB. If the board could have been a little more flexible and patient, the Bible school could have had all the water they needed. As they say, "Hindsight is 20/20."

As time went on, the college began experiencing some growing pains at the new campus in Lewistown. With a new college name, new location, and a new student load, problems began surfacing.

The campus was located a good number of miles out from a small town so not everyone could find jobs. As time went on, students were forced to withdraw from their programs—resulting in a loss of student revenue. Then there were the wicked winters and icy roads that plagued Maiden Valley. Food trucks and other services could not deliver their loads to the campus kitchen due to a snowbound road that the State of Montana did not plow.

The Big Sky Bible College eventually folded. Several years later, a small number of concerned folks wanted to make a new start, and they started a new Bible school in Bozeman, which they named Montana Bible College.

Several years later, the former students of MIB/BSBC began referring to themselves as "survivors." Even though it's a catchy name, I purposely have refused to be labeled a MIB Survivor. Why? In all the years I have been a professional counselor and chaplain, it has always been my ministry to move people onward, forward, and upward. I've worked to help transition their thinking from being mere survivors to becoming thrivers.

I can understand folks wanting to be identified with that catchy term survivor. But words and titles can create negative connotations in how we see ourselves, and how others view us. The decisions and choices we make in life, whether good or bad, can follow us for the next forty years—or a lifetime.

When poor decisions and choices are made, they often make one feel empty, impotent, inadequate, and helpless. In my first book, The Whirlwind Principle: Bringing the Calm to the Storms of Life, I call this particular area "the regrets of life."

When you make bad decisions, it fast-forwards you into making bad choices, which pushes you into making a bad move, sending you into the regret zone. This is when you feel stuck.

The regret zone is not a friendly place to be visiting. It gives off the foul air of trouble. In this zone the future is unknown and stormy days lie ahead. When our circumstances are in total chaos, life is uncomfortable and frustrating.

At this point, instead of zigzagging, we begin to feel like our circumstances are out of control, making us feel like we're zagging.

Have you noticed that you can always pick out the zaggers?

They are the ones who complain about their many troubles. They are the ones who have shot themselves in the foot, and are standing back admiring their aim.

When I counsel these individuals, I try to move them forward, onward, and upward to get them out of their stuck state of mind.

I would venture to say most of the survivor folks' zigzagging moments were created by choosing the wrong friends to hang out with, or even marrying one of those misguided folks. This has led to sleepless nights, and the endless pacing of empty floors, trying to figure out an alternative to their problems.

The trouble with trouble, is that it is troubling—even if someone is saved.

Trouble and problems are the building blocks of life. Many of life's lessons are learned through those zigzags.

Africans have a unique term for zigzags. In Swahili, the term is mabonde na mlima, pronounced: (ma bo-day na ma-lay-ma), meaning "mountains and valleys."

The truth of the matter is, I have been there—and so have you!

In fact, there have been times when I felt more like I was zagging than zigging. Nothing seemed to be working out for me and everything was wrong. It wasn't until I could get alone and begin praying, or get with a trusted and competent friend that I could slowly begin to move out of some of those zigzagging moments.

"The slap of a friend can be trusted to help you, but the kisses of an enemy are nothing but lies" (1 Cor. 10:13 MSG).

Chapter Three Review
Zigging or Zagging

Discussion:

The things that are hurled at us in life help focus us to become thrivers, not merely survivors.

1. Why was dodgeball so important to those who participated?
2. How did dodgeball prepare me for the military—and for life?
3. We all face red–rubber ball encounters. Can you share one you've experienced?
4. How can Scripture benefit those faced with being attacked?
5. Explain in your own words the difference between a survivor and a thriver.

Goal Setting

What are some goals you would like to achieve as you have read chapter three?

_____

_____

_____

_____

_____

CHAPTER FOUR

Zig Zag Challenges

I t all began one early summer morning on July 16, 1982 when I received a call from Tri-County Metropolitan Transit Company in Portland, Oregon informing me I was hired on as a bus operator. That phone call made my day!

The first year of working for this bus company was a honeymoon experience. But not long afterward, things begin to get considerably less glamorous. Reality set in, and it didn't take long for me to figure out that this job was going to be a demanding one.

I was in my last year at Western Conservative Baptist Theological Seminary in Portland. Kathy and I were managing apartments to help with extra money needed for my tuition.

Some of my classmates were already driving for this bus company. They had nothing but great things to say about their jobs. They were classified as "mini-bus" operators, meaning they were part-time, and only allowed to drive four-to-six-hour day shifts. Driving the morning and evening rush hours gave them the necessary time to attend classes during midday. They even had weekends off.

The more I learned about this bus driving job, the more interested I became, so I went down to apply. Next thing I knew, I

---

found myself in a two-week training course learning how to drive a transit bus through the streets of Portland.

It seemed to be a perfect fit for me. Not only could Kathy and I live on the money I was making, but we could easily pay our school bills. We had planned that I would stay employed for eight months until I graduated. All we ever wanted after graduation was to take a rural pastorate with horses and a few cows in our back acres. It was the perfect plan! Or so I thought.

My plan was short lived. It got quickly interrupted when I was approached by our station manager at the bus company asking if I would sign up to be a voluntary chaplain to the employees of the bus company, since he knew I was due to graduate from seminary.

He thought this position would be a perfect fit for me, as well as for the company. There were a good number of drivers who were experiencing a high rate of divorce, and others had family troubles that affected their performance at work.

After discussing the idea of becoming a transit chaplain with my wife, I took the position. Why am I telling you all of these stories about this particular bus company? It's because I want to drive home a basic principle: A doesn't always lead to B. Even with the best of intentions, the best of planning, even with much prayer, A will not always lead an individual to B.

On the job I found it interesting when I learned that there were a good number of fellow bus drivers who had college degrees. In fact, many of them had their teaching certificates. The former teachers had all traded in their classrooms for a job driving a bulky, forty-foot long city bus. I found it totally unbelievable!

Many of them were driving more than 150 miles per day through the heart of Portland in some of the most challenging traffic, and interacting with more than 800-plus bus passengers on a daily basis.

It was equally surprising when one of the drivers said she had always wanted a challenge in life, and teaching a bunch of noisy, undisciplined kids simply did not give her that thrill. She bragged about always making the dean's list with her excellent grades, and had graduated cum laude, and received one of the highest honors at her graduation exercises. She was offered a full-time teaching position at an elite teaching institution in her state.

After spending all that time, effort, and money to arrive at her goal, she stepped into a screaming classroom only to learn she could not tolerate or handle all the drama and chaos. So she quit.

As a result, she sat unemployed and totally frustrated for about six months until she read in the newspaper about the local city bus company hiring bus drivers. When she read that they even provided training, she applied.

To her surprise, sitting in the hot seat of a city bus gave her the satisfaction and fulfillment she was looking for. She was gifted at doing it, and it paid extremely well. Once she got hired on as a full-time bus operator, she informed me she was making four times the salary she was getting as a school teacher.

There were other employees who shared similar stories. A chiropractor gave up his practice to come and join the bus transit family. He simply felt inadequate and totally unsatisfied with his chiropractic career. He, too, quit and became one of our best bus operators.

But one of the frustrating issues of my employment was getting along with the public. The company simply did not put up with complaints. This was at a time when transit companies did not care about employees' "feelings." They only cared about keeping their company rolling along, and keeping the demanding bus schedules on time. Anything more was considered a personal problem.

So whatever the bus operator faced at work, they would most certainly take those difficulties home to their families. This thankless position not only placed a lot of undue stress on me and the other bus operators, but also made it impossible to go home happy.

What kept us coming to work each day was the incredible financial incentive program, which kept the driver focused on making more money. It was a program I called: "chasing the carrot."

The "carrot" program was a success in its own way, because I spent twenty-four years there. In 2006, I retired with full benefits (including medical coverage for the rest of my life). This incentive program not only helped me pay off all my educational degrees, but it also provided our family with an upper-middle class living in upper-scale neighborhoods and driving new vehicles. I traded my time for a healthy paycheck. There is a term for this: transactionalism.

Remember, A doesn't always lead to B. There will be detours and interruptions along the way.

Just reread Exodus 13:17–22. If you remember, Moses was sent to deliver the people of God. The only problem was that God had other plans than taking this disorganized group of people in a straight line from A to B.

Israel had been in captivity for hundreds of years when God sovereignly raised up this guy named Moses to lead His people out of captivity.

The interesting truth about this whole saga is that God purposely led this group of people on a crooked path—a crisscross pattern—throughout their journey to the Promise Land.

Their journey is described by the zigzag principle. Why? Because these folks had been held in captivity over a long period of time and had developed an inferiority complex. They were brainwashed by a wicked king called a pharaoh and were stuck in their dreadful circumstances. They had lost their confidence to think for themselves, and didn't trust anyone, including the guy sent to deliver them.

Pharaoh thought he had them duped. They were stuck under his evil power. He had succeeded in short-circuiting their confidence, making them feel impotent.

Almighty God knew their shortcomings when He said, "Then it came to pass, when Pharaoh had let the people go, that God did not lead them by way of the land of the Philistines, although that was near; for God said, 'Lest perhaps the people change their minds when they see war, and return to Egypt'" (Ex. 13:17 NKJV).

The words "to change their minds," means to be overcome by anxiety and depression. Fearing the unknown, they were simply a spooked people. There is nothing more draining on one's mind than not knowing the future. Or even worse, is not knowing what is going to happen just around the corner in our lives.

A fear of the unknown is a dreadful feeling of being alone and lost. I call it a "slave mentality." It paralyzes our ability to think straight. It strangles our thoughts, causing us to think irrationally, and not trust ourselves.

Thriver or Survivor?

The children of Israel were victims of their own circumstances. Instead of becoming overcomers, they settled for being survivors. Survivors would rather endure the known pain, rather than deal with the unknown. They normally are people who are stuck in life. They lack passion and purpose. If these folks could learn to step out of their shells and take a little risk, they could learn to move forward in life and become thrivers.

Thrivers grow vigorously. They flourish, blooming and blossoming where they are planted. They prosper, succeed, and increase in whatever life throws at them.

Don't forget, when we accept Christ as Savior, we still maintain a carnal nature. When we get out of sorts and have bad days, there is a good possibility that we too act like the Israelites stuck in captivity and not knowing the future. We, too, can walk in the flesh, seeking for shortcuts, and a way out of our problems.

This is why it's important to understand that zigzags give us an opportunity to slow down so we can keep our footing on solid ground and follow in the footsteps of Jesus Christ.

If you are stuck in the unknown and trying to figure your way out of your circumstances, today might just be your day to lose your slave mentality. Quit walking in the flesh, and turn to Jesus to help you get freed from your captivity of sin.

In your zigzagging moments, you need to know a couple of truths to help you onward in your spiritual journey.

First, straight lines do not exist on your spiritual journeys with the Lord. Those zigzags are given to help you make it through life a little safer by slowing you down, and enabling you to refocus.

Second, your focus determines your direction. Remember: If you aim at nothing, you will hit it.

In Romans 8:28–39, the apostle Paul gives us a road map to successful living when he talks about divine interruptions—that's right, the zigzags of life. Paul is pumping truth into the brains of the Roman Christians when he writes about eternal life.

His theme is that we can be confident that God will sovereignly keep us secure in Jesus Christ, in spite of our circumstances (good or bad). Now that's a lot of security. That should brighten up anyone's day!

Dr. Grant Howard, in his book *The Trauma of Transparency*,[1] says, "Even in the midst of personal anxiety, God wants us to accentuate the positive and tell Him we are thankful not only for the events of our lives but also for our relationship with the God who is in control of the events (1 Thess. 5:18; Rom. 8:28)."

That thought alone should give us confidence to face a precarious, chaotic world. The reason? Almighty God is in complete control. So cheer up! Go ahead and take a deep breath—and relax. According to this theological truth, God is majestically sovereign and in control of our circumstances.

---

[1] J. Grant Howard, *The Trauma of Transparency* (Colorado Springs: Multnomah Press), 132.

Charles H. Spurgeon, one of our most respected preachers of the past once said, "Many men owe the grandeur of their lives to their tremendous difficulties."[2]

That puts life into perspective, doesn't it? The apostle Paul continues on his theme of God's majestic sovereignty in Romans 8:28–39 by showing how He is in control, even during the rough moments in life.

Paul give us three crystal-clear biblical facts:

Fact #1—God Does the Calling (Rom. 8:17–20)

When I think of God's plan for His people, Psalm 139 pops up on my radar screen. King David asked the question: "Can you go anywhere away from God?" Psalm 139 assures you and me that the answer is an unequivocal "No!"

No one can outrun the living God—no one! There is simply not a place on Planet Earth where you can escape the presence of God. He is Emmanuel—God with us. This means He is present everywhere, and is involved in all of our circumstances.

Sometimes living in the fast lane of life may blur our vision about the zigzags that God has sovereignly placed in our pathways. Consider them as just speed bumps to help slow us down.

That's why straight lines don't work for the most part. Straight lines are a recipe for careless and reckless living. Staying in the ruts of those zigzags only causes us to pay better attention. Remember, focus determines your direction.

He Chose Us

In Paul's letter to the Romans, it is clear God elected His people. Elected is from the Greek word eklego, simply meaning "to pick out or choose for oneself." The apostle Paul speaks about this word when he wrote: "Long before he laid down earth's foundations, he

---

[2] Nelson L. Price, *Shadows We Run From* (Nashville: Broadman Press, 1975), 68.

had us in mind, had settled on us as the focus of his love, to be made whole and holy by his love. Long, long ago he decided to adopt us into his family through Jesus Christ. (What pleasure he took in planning this!) He wanted us to enter into the celebration of his lavish gift-giving by the hand of his beloved Son" (Eph. 1:4–6 MSG).

Election is a big theological word, and it can come across as being intimidating if one is not familiar with its meaning. But in layman's language, it simply means: "God's gracious plan before creation to save those who believe."

Back in my New Testament Theology class in seminary, Dr. Cook put it this way: "Election is that phase of God's eternal purpose (decree) whereby He certainly and eternally determines, by means of unconditional and loving choice, who will believe. It is not mere purpose to give salvation to those who may believe, but rather it determines who will believe."[3]

After graduating from seminary back in the 1980s, I did a lot of pulpit supply. I was sent to preach a Sunday morning message at a church where the pastor was absent. I really loved being in different churches, in different cities, preaching the Word of God to a fresh audience.

One church in western Washington State stands out in my memory. As I entered the sanctuary, I noticed a wooden sign that hung above the door that said, "Whosoever Will May Come." As I stepped inside the sanctuary, I looked back and was surprised to see another wooden sign that read "Chosen in Him From Before the Foundation of the World."

Those two wooden signs really made a gigantic impact on me that morning. The first sign spoke of the availability of salvation; while the second sign spoke of the fact of God's choosing.

---

[3] Dr. W. Robert Cook, New Testament Theology class notes, Western Seminary, Portland, Oregon, 1981, 38.

Both those wooden signs were theologically right on. They pointed to a profound truth: If God had not sovereignly elected His chosen people, none would have believed.

The apostle Paul uses additional words to describe God's loyal love to His people. One of those words is "foreknew," from the Greek word proginosko.

Dr. Earl Radmacker, former president of Western Seminary in Portland, writes about this theological word. He says, "A common view of the words 'whom He foreknew' is that by foresight God saw the faith by which some would believe. The problem with this view is that the object of foreknowledge in Romans 8:29 is not a person's faith but is a person ("whom"). That is, God foreknew the person, not something he or she would do. This is consistent with the determining action in the other links of the chain right on to glorification."[4]

Dr. Radmacker points out that the word foreknew (proginosko) is also found in Acts 26:5 and 2 Peter 3:17. He goes on to explain that the term found in Romans 8:28 shows that God, not man, is the active agent from beginning to end.

According to Dr. Radmacker, those whom God elected He engaged in a conscious, loving relationship. That is what Romans 8:28 is trying to communicate to the Roman believer—and to you and me!

This is why you and I can remain calm in a chaotic world. Christ has given us the confidence that He is the Alpha and Omega, and life begins and ends with Him.

Personally, this particular word totally excites me! It gives the incredible message that almighty God is totally trustworthy and reliable in our troubled world, filled with all kinds of dangers and heartaches. The point Paul makes is clear: We are His, and He belongs to us.

---

[4] Earl Radmacker, *Salvation* (Nashville, Tenn.: Word Publishing, 2000) 29.

Another interesting word is "predestination." Earl Radmacker explains the word in the Greek simply means "to mark off with a boundary beforehand."

In other words, God preplanned a great destiny for those who have a personal relationship with Him. That means, over time, we as believers would begin to conform in our spiritual walks into the image of Jesus Christ. The apostle Paul writes on this truth when he penned the following words: "In him we were also chosen, having been predestined according to the plan of him who works out everything in conformity with the purpose of his will" (Eph. 1:11 NIV).

John picks up the theme by writing: "Beloved, we are God's children now, and what we will be has not yet appeared; but we know that when He appears we shall be like him, because we shall see him as he is" (1 John 3:2 ESV).

Here's the bottom line. Those who trust and accept Jesus Christ by faith are members of God's great family. Knowing we are not only conforming into the image of the Lord Jesus Christ, but that we will spend eternity in Heaven with Him, should make our day. When it's time to be called home to heaven, there will be one gigantic celebration no one will want to miss out on!

Believers can relax as God is majestically sovereign and in complete control.

Incidentally, there are other important words—like "chosen" and "called"—that can be added to the list.

The meaning of these words may not mean a whole lot to some, but to the Christian, they mean everything. I am His, and He is mine! Simple stuff, but profoundly rich in meaning.

Those profound words point to the truth that God not only redeemed us from the slave camps of sin, but that He reconciled us to Himself. He even forgave all of our sins.

Fact #2 God Does the Protecting (Rom. 8:31–34)

Christ's death, burial, and resurrection are the believer's security. This is what I call the work of the Son of God in action. I say this because it means the believer has been "justified." Justification is God's act of removing the guilt and penalty of sin while at the same time declaring a sinner righteous through Christ's atoning sacrifice. That is why Paul can say with complete confidence: "Who shall lay any thing to the charge of God's elect?" (Rom. 8:33 KJV). Paul answers his own question in the same breath when he proclaims: "It is God that justifies."

Paul continues his argument for total security for the believer in Romans 8:33–35 (NIV). "Who will bring any charge against those whom God has chosen? It is God who justifies. Who then is the one who condemns? No one. Christ Jesus who died—more than that, who was raised to life—is at the right hand of God and is also interceding for us. Who shall separate us from the love of Christ? Shall trouble or hardship or persecution or famine or nakedness or danger or sword?"

Here's my point: Anyone who has believed on Jesus has already been justified. See for yourselves (Rom. 3:26, 6:7, 8:30). These verses pull out this truth very clearly.

We need to bear in mind that Christ died on the cross in our place. That's rock bottom theology.

Furthermore, Jesus Christ, was raised by resurrection power and now sits on the right hand of God making intercession for you and me.

Bible scholar, Dr. Lewis Sperry Chafer, wrote, "A justification which is not subject to human merit could hardly be subject to human demerit."

Dr. Robert Cook, my old theology professor, said this about justification in a class in 1982: "Romans 8:34 makes it clear that if someone is to be condemned, it must be Christ, for it is on Him, not man, that salvation rests in the first place. Anything that affects the believer affects Him, because we are united to Him. Since this is true, any blame for defection from faith, the loss of eternal life by any child of God, would rest in Christ Jesus."

I am awfully grateful that I personally have a protector, Jesus Christ, whom I can totally rely upon. He is the One who:

- Sustains (Rom. 8:31)
- Justifies (Rom. 8:32–33)
- Condemns (Rom. 8:34).

If these three theological truths are factual, then you and I should have total confidence in the resurrected Savior that our salvation is complete and safe. So relax! Our God Jehovah is majestically sovereign and in control.

Fact #3 God Does the Securing (Rom. 8:35–39)

Romans 8 is just as relevant today as it was when it was written back in AD 56. Paul explains the word salvation by asking, "Who shall separate us from the love of Christ? Shall trouble or hardship or persecution or famine or nakedness or danger or sword?" (Rom. 8:35 NIV). Almost in the same breath, the apostle Paul answers his own question "We are more than conquerors through him who loved us" (v. 37).

The context of this scriptural passage centers around the love of Christ. God's love is so amazing! He had me in mind when Christ died for my sins on the cross of Calvary. That is some amazing love!

It was Christ's resurrection power that came to rescue— deliver—to save—those who answer the call of salvation. Jesus redeemed—paid the price—for all. The all are those individuals who call upon His name by faith, asking Him to save them.

Without the cross, there is no salvation. This is why it is difficult to understand why there are those who hold to the view that a saved individual can be lost.

When challenged to prove this from the Word, those same individuals often give the same answer: "It is sin that unsaves a Christian."

Unsaves?

Here's the truth, regardless of one's race, color, age, or status, anyone saved can reach heaven.

The issue is not a sinless life, but rather, a personal trust in Christ alone on the basis of faith. Therefore, salvation is the key to eternal life, not whether someone sinned or not.

"Remember that a man who keeps the whole Law but for a single exception is none the less a law-breaker" (James 2:10 Phillips).

God did not distinguish between the big and little sins. Sin is sin, period! If our salvation rests upon the omniscience of God, then where is there room for "falling from grace"?

If almighty God knew you or I would fall from grace after we were saved—ultimately making us lost—then why would He have chosen to save us in the first place? There is something incongruent about this.

I believe the omniscience of God is an unassailable argument for eternal security for all those who place their trust in Christ alone for their salvation.

God's immutability proves He never changes His mind. James 1:17 (NASB) supports this truth: "Every good thing given and every perfect gift is from above, coming down from the Father of lights, with whom there is no variation or shifting shadow."

I view the security of the saints this way: If God is sovereign, believers are totally secure, for they are in His loving care as Lord and Savior. And, if God is omnipresent, then there is no place I can go to escape from the presence of God.

In the midst of our zigzags, God is there to keep us safe in

His hands—and protect us from all evil. That is probably the best security anyone could possibly have.

Paul again answers this concern when he writes: "My sheep hear My voice, and I know them, and they follow Me; and I give eternal life to them, and they will never perish; and no one will snatch them out of My hand. My Father, who has given them to Me, is greater than all; and no one is able to snatch them out of the Father's hand" (John 10:27–29 NASB).

What I love about this particular passage of Scripture, is that it speaks about Christ's protection. As much as a shepherd protects his own sheep, Jesus protects His people from eternal harm.

Dr. W. Robert Cook, former professor of theology at Western Conservative Baptist Seminary in Portland, wrote: "Christ's intention is to leave believers in the world while preserving them from the evil one. John appeals to this same truth with somewhat different terminology in 1 John 5:18 (NASB). 'He who was born of God [Jesus Christ] keeps him [the believer] and the evil one does not touch him.'"[5]

The point is, Christ cares for His own. According to Romans 8:34, Christ sits at the right hand of God, and He intercedes for His own. Hebrews 7:25 (NASB) says, "Therefore He is able to save forever those who draw near to God through Him, since He always lives to make intercession for them."

The Scriptures show us that Christ has a deep love for His own. This does not mean that Christ is unconcerned about the unsaved. He is! Listen to His concern: "'Father, forgive these people,' Jesus said, 'for they don't know what they are doing'" (Luke 23:34 TLB).

---

[5] Robert W. Cook, *The Theology of John* (Chicago: Moody Publishing, 1979) 168–169.

Chapter Four Review
Zigzag Challenges

Discussion:

My new job as a transit operator in the city of Portland, Oregon was my dream job with great pay. I learned many lessons during my employment with this company—some good and some bad. Zigzag moments on a job can be difficult.

1. What challenges have you experienced at work?
2. Name a few ways working with the public can be difficult.
3. Discuss my statement: "A does not always lead to B."
4. Read Romans 8:28–29 and discuss why it is so important for the believer.
5. Can you give another Bible verse proving God's deep love and protection for His children?

Goal Setting

What are some goals you would like to achieve as you have read chapter four?

_____

_____

_____

_____

_____

CHAPTER FIVE

Zigzag Realities

There is nothing worse than feeling as if you are isolated in your own little world or all alone on a remote island in the middle of Nowhere Land.

If we live long enough, there will always be low moments (valleys) that will occupy our minds and rob our peace.

Even the apostle Paul at one point in his ministry entered one of these zigzag moments he describes in 2 Corinthians 1:8–11 (Phillips).

> We should like you, our brothers, to know something of what we went through in Asia. At that time we were completely overwhelmed, the burden was more than we could bear, in fact we told ourselves that this was the end. Yet we believe now that we had this experience of coming to the end of our tether that we might learn to trust, not in ourselves, but in God who can raise the dead. It was God who preserved us from imminent death, and it is he who still preserves us. Further, we trust him to

keep us safe in the future, and here you can join in and help by praying for us, so that the good that is done to us in answer to many prayers will mean eventually that many will thank God for our preservation.

Pain Brings Gain

Sometimes people just have to experience pain—a lot of pain—before they have a reality check.

That reminds me of the prodigal son, a young energetic man who wanted his dad to settle up with him. He wanted to fly the coop, take his money, and run off to a foreign land. While there, he spends everything on wine, women, and song. It doesn't take long for him to lose his inheritance. He ends up feeding hogs—and eating what they eat—but eventually comes to his senses and goes home to his father.

In counseling, I've seen how pain brings gain.

Several years ago, I informed Rick (not his real name), a father of two little boys, that his marriage was in trouble.

"Mind your own business," he told me.

Since he was bigger than me, I followed his advice.

But one afternoon I had a phone call saying, "Dr. Tom, this is Rick. I'm being arrested."

I asked, "What are they charging you with?"

"I assaulted my wife."

"How did you assault her?"

He seemed embarrassed as he replied. "I've been suspecting that she has been having an affair, and when I confronted her, she threw her new iPhone at me assuming I didn't know how to use it. But I had just upgraded my old phone to an iPhone, and knew exactly how to open her phone. I started to check her messages.

"She quickly tried to grab it out of my hands as I pivoted. She missed the phone and ended up ripping my shirt half off and scraping the side of my face, drawing blood with her sharp nails."

I told him, "Relax! You are a lucky man! It will be your wife who will be arrested, not you!" Sure enough, the police came, saw his injury and torn shirt, and arrested her.

The next day, Rick became a counseling client and we were able to not only save their marriage, and get them back together as a family, about six months later.

Here's the point: Sometimes people are not motivated to seek help until they hurt enough.

When Trouble Comes

The apostle Paul affirms, "For God sometimes uses sorrow in our lives to help us turn away from sin and seek eternal life. We should never regret His sending it . . ." (2 Cor. 7:10 TLB).

Job, in the Old Testament, knew something about trouble. He said, "But mankind is born for trouble as surely as sparks fly upward" (Job 5:7 HCSB).

King David, who also experienced many difficulties, said, "The good man does not escape all troubles—he has them too. But the Lord helps him in each and every one" (Ps. 34:19 TLB).

The truths we can learn from the lives of Job and King David are sobering. Troubles cannot be avoided. They are what they are.

However, there is good news! The Bible provides hope for when we are caught in the zigzags of life.

Psalm 13 is a classic example of this truth. King David gives a peek through the windows of his own zigzag moment in his painful plea to God.

> How long, O Yahweh?
> Will You forget me forever?
> How long
> Will you hide Your face from me?
> How long

Having grief in my heart continually?
How long
Will my enemy be exalted over me?
Show regard! Answer me!
O Yahweh my God!
Enlighten my eyes,
Lest I sleep the sleep of death;
Lest my enemy say, "I have prevailed against Him,"
Lest my adversaries rejoice because I am shaken.
But I, trust in Your loyal love;
My heart shall rejoice in Your salvation.
I will certainly sing to Yahweh,
Because He deals bountifully with me.
(Ps. 13:1–6 author's paraphrase[1])

King David paints a descriptive picture of defeat in this passage of Scripture. You can feel the pain of his agony as you read these words. He's totally devastated and has come to the end of his rope. His courage is gone. Yet David doesn't lose his trust in God's loyal love, and he actively praises Him.

Perhaps you may feel like David—empty, alone, like no one cares. Maybe you feel you have no one to turn to. Trust God's loyal love.

Hitting Bottom

A middle-aged woman bus operator was walking out of the "bullpen" at the transit company as I was coming into the building one early morning. When we encountered each other at the door, I could tell there was something wrong as she seemed visibly upset.

She started speaking to me and then simply lost it as tears began streaming down her red cheeks. She then passed me a note

---

[6] Author's paraphrase based on the *Biblia Hebraica Stuttgartensia* (Stuttgart, Germany: Bibelstiftung, 1967/77).

she had written on a napkin at 4:00 a.m. that morning. I read these sobering words: "I have been discouraged for so long, I have lost my will to live."

She began crying harder and placed her head on my shoulders, and then she began wailing. It was obvious she had hit bottom. Her world had caved in.

I knew she was in no shape to be driving a forty-foot transit bus with passengers on board that morning. I escorted her from the bullpen into a quiet unoccupied room where no one else could see her. I then got her off from her bus run.

As she told me her story, I listened without interruption. During the telling she'd burst into uncontrollable sobs.

Afterwards I offered her hope, trying to stabilize her troubled mind, and helped her make an appointment with her medical doctor.

It took several months of healing, but eventually she was able to return back to work with a smile on her face. Later she agreed to help me make a video introducing our chaplaincy program.

There is nothing worse than experiencing the kind of defeat and depression that robs us of positive and healthy thoughts. We feel isolated, aloof, distant from family and friends, and as if no one cares.

There will be rainy days and low moments in life. Expect them to creep in, causing chaos and sadness.

Let's be real! We live in an imperfect world, and we are imperfect individuals. We get worn out, hungry, and at times moody. Sometimes we just need to step back and take a break.

Going Through Low Points

In my first book, *The Whirlwind Principle: Bringing the Calm to the Storms of Life,* I mentioned Habakkuk and King David in the Old Testament. They were men of God, wonderful leaders, and yet, even they were plagued with low points in their lives. Both struggled with their own troubles. How do we know that? Because they wrote transparently about their troubles and their thoughts were recorded in the Old Testament.

Habakkuk complained that everything was wrong with his ministry. He felt lonely, drained of his joy in serving His Lord. He cried out for help—"O Lord!"

To his surprise, there was no answer at first. Here are his sobering words as he cries out to the living God, as recorded in Habakkuk 1:1–4 (ESV).

> O Lord, how long shall I cry for help,
>   and you will not hear?
> Or cry to you "Violence!"
>   and you will not save?
> Why do you make me see iniquity,
>   and why do you idly look at wrong?
> Destruction and violence are before me;
>   strife and contention arise.
> So the law is paralyzed,
>   and justice never goes forth.
> For the wicked surround the righteous;
>   so justice goes forth perverted.

In another translation, we see the pain of Habakkuk's plaintive cries. Each word is a genuine cry for the helping hand of the living God.

> O Lord, how long must I call for help before you will listen? I shout to You in vain; there is no answer. "Help! Murder!" I cry, but no one comes to save. Must I forever see this sin and sadness all around me? Wherever I look there is oppression and bribery and men who

love to argue and to fight. The law is not enforced and there is no justice given in the courts, for the wicked far outnumber the righteous, and bribes and trickery prevail. (Hab. 1:2–4 TLB)

It is not until later in chapter three that we see God dealing graciously and mercifully with Habakkuk. As a result, we find the complaining prophet singing and rejoicing about how Yahweh cared for him and his ministry.

When God Seems Far Away

Then the Bible gives us a glimpse of the struggles and sorrows of King David. David complained that there was no way around his troubles. Even though he prayed like Habakkuk and poured his heart out to the living God, he felt abandoned by God.

David's pain and agony can be felt through the magnificent words of Psalm 13. In this psalm we have a peek into King David's life, showing us a servant-leader who is sorely tried by persecutions and sufferings.

I've been there—so have you! I can tell you there have been times that I felt more like I was zagging rather than zigging through some of my circumstances. We all have those terrible moments when nothing seems to be working right, and everything is in chaos. We can be at rock bottom, or going through tough times that nobody, including our family or friends, knows anything about.

I want to be like King David and Habakkuk in praying and asking God for help.

Psalm 13 is a beautiful piece of wisdom literature written in poetic form. It came alive for me as I read it. I think an appropriate title would be "When God Seems Far Away." The subject of the text seems to scream out discouragement.

David's theme at the end of the passage is also profound: God's loyal love is always present in the time of need. David's aim seems to be to encourage those struggling with their personal zigzags not to give up. God is present—He has not forgotten you!

With those encouraging words, David then gives the big idea of his argument. If his main thought could be put into a phrase that speaks volumes in our 21st century lives, I think it would be "negative thinking is a choice."

Negative Thinking Is a Choice

How did King David know negative thinking is a choice? We see in the psalm that David begins to think that he is forgotten and forsaken by God. Yes, David personally went through many trials and much emotional pain. But he discovered God was with him the entire time. God had not gone off anywhere. David was not forgotten. His words in Psalm 13 give us heavenly insight and hope.

Here's the big question: How can we find relief in a negative world, knowing that negative thinking is a choice?

The answer is found in three truths found in Psalm 13. Let's look at the first truth.

#1 Put Aside Doubt

First, we must put aside doubt (Ps. 13:1–2). Webster's New World Dictionary defines doubt as "to waiver in opinion or belief. To be uncertain or undecided; to be inclined to disbelief; to have no trust or confidence in."

Do you doubt God is with you? Do you ever feel as if He is aloof and doesn't care?

The truth is, God has not forgotten any of us.

That reminds me of the true story Dr. J. Carl Laney, one of my seminary professors, told in chapel one day. He said a well-known professor from a popular seminary had been a few hundred miles away from home speaking at a week-long series of meetings. After the week was over, the professor flew back to his city, and took a cab to his house. When he got to the door his wife asked, "But, where is the car, honey? Did you forget you drove this time?"

This brilliant professor had forgotten! He had to take the same taxi back to the airport and return to get his forgotten car.

Forgetfulness is a people kind of thing. It is not a trait unique to absentminded professors; we all forget at times. But God never forgets.

Psalm 13 is a poem that has three movements to it, each consisting of two verses. The first movement is a four-fold chant of "How long?" It says, "How long, O LORD? Will you forget me forever? How long will you hide your face from me? How long must I wrestle with my thoughts and every day have sorrow in my heart? How long will my enemy triumph over me?" (Ps. 13:1–2 NIV).

Read those words slowly. Do you feel the agonizing pain of David's plaintive cry? The psalmist chants: *"How long? . . . how long? . . . how long? . . . how long?"* These plaintive cries are the impassioned words of one who believes himself truly forgotten by God.

It is interesting that the Hebrew words translated "how long?" evoke a picture of a man who is lost in deep unforgiving, forsaken jungles of a foreign land. He is lost with no food or water and is aware that his strength is giving out with all the forces of jungle life closing in on him.

It is not until this lost man reaches a high point of the jungle, and looks out over the jungle of trees, that he sees where he needs to be to find his way out of his impossible predicament.

Sometimes in our own little jungles of life, we, too, can feel the way David did. We want a way out! And we want it *now!* When God doesn't answer right away, we begin to assume He has forgotten about us and forsaken us.

We are not alone in feeling this way. How do I know that?

Let's look at the big picture in Psalm 13. In it I see help for people stuck in the zigzagging moments of life. We see in these six profound verses that King David was miserable—zagging his way through life.

It wasn't until David finally came to his senses that he discovered that almighty God was actually involved in his life, and that Yahweh would lead him out of his bad moments. His revelation took him to a new level of thinking about God, and how God makes Himself available to His people.

David was able to put down those negative thoughts, realizing he had a choice in the matter. And that's the theme of Psalm 13—people have a choice in how they respond to their circumstances.

This brings us to the second truth.

#2 Ask for Assistance (Ps. 13:3–4)

Believe it or not, God never intended you (or anyone else) to get stuck in endlessly zigzagging moments. Jesus affirmed: "The thief's purpose is to steal, kill and destroy. My purpose is to give life in all its fullness" (John 10:10 TLB).

Problems, disappointments, and trials will come and go. They just exist in our daily lives—they just are! We need to learn to cry out for assistance during those precarious moments in life. Otherwise, our peace of mind will be eaten away. Jesus said, "Come to me, all of you who are weary and over-burdened, and I will give you rest!" (Matt. 11:28 Phillips).

God wants to be involved with our lives. He desires our prayers, petitions, and time. You will never wear out your welcome with Him . . . *never*! The Bible is quick to point this out in Hebrews 4:16 (Phillips): "Let us therefore approach the throne of grace with fullest confidence, that we may receive mercy for our failures and grace to help in the hour of need."

Proverbs 3:5–6 (hcsb) says, "Trust in the Lord with all your heart, and do not rely on your own understanding; think about Him in all your ways, and He will guide you on the right paths."

David is quick to point out that people are prone to forget God and sometimes leave Him altogether out of the picture of their lives. "Look on me and answer, O Lord my God. Give light to my eyes, or I will sleep in death; my enemy will say, 'I have overcome him, and my foes will rejoice when I fall'" (Ps. 13:3–4 NIV).

In the second movement of this psalm, David reminds the reader to pray and worship God—allowing Him to show His love and power in running to our rescue.

That brings us to the third truth.

#3 Trust Yahweh (Ps. 13:5–6)

David begins this third movement by saying, "But I, in Your loyal love, I trust" (Ps. 13:5, author's translation from the Hebrew). The New International Version of verses 5–6 reads, "But I trust in your unfailing love; my heart rejoices in your salvation. I will sing to the LORD, for he has been good to me."

The point of this whole movement hinges on the Hebrew word *dsh* (*hesed*, reading the word from backward to forward). Hesed in the Hebrew is translated "the loyal love of Yahweh."

The point of this Hebrew translation is that in Yahweh's loyal love there is no forgetting.

When our two children were small, I would sometimes play with them too roughly, forgetting that they were small and fragile. Then they'd run to their mommy and cry.

Kathy reminded me, "Don't play so rough with them. They're just little." She reminded me that they needed me to be tender, merciful, and a loving father—otherwise they might grow up thinking I was a monster.

The very next day after we had talked about this, the word

hesed was introduced to my Hebrew class in seminary. I sat there listening raptly to every word Dr. Allen was teaching.

The light came on when I learned the word meant the loyal love of God. God cannot, and will not, forget who we are. I could not wait to get home and teach our Scott and Pamela this word.

Here's how it worked.

When we would be playing and roughhousing, if I would forget how small and fragile they really were, they would yell, "Hesed, Daddy." No matter where we were in our play, Daddy would stop! They learned to trust me. They quickly found out by using that very important word that their Daddy would not hurt them or forget their frailty.

God in His Sovereignty is the very same way with you and me. He wants us to cry out to Him when life becomes too difficult to handle. We are to cry, "Hesed."

Learn that word. Say it repeatedly. It is one of the most important theological words you will ever learn in the Hebrew.

Maybe that is why King David could place such confidence in God even when He seemed so very far away. He trusted in the hesed—the loyal love of God.

Let's look at Habakkuk 3:17–19 (TLB) for an important point we can learn.

> Even though the fig trees are all destroyed, and there is neither blossom left nor fruit; though the olive crops all fail, and the fields lie barren; even if the flocks die in the fields and the cattle barns are empty, yet I will rejoice in the Lord; I will be happy in the God of my salvation. The Lord God is my strength; he will give me the speed of a deer and bring me safely over the mountains.

These verses say we can rejoice in God, our salvation and

strength, even when the worst happens. He will "bring me safely over the mountains."

Another verse, 2 Timothy 2:13 (Phillips) in the New Testament, reminds us of the loyal love and faithfulness of God when it says, "If we died with him we shall also live with him: if we suffer we shall also reign with him. If we deny him he will also deny us: yet if we are faithless he always remains faithful. He cannot deny his own nature."

As we wind up Psalm 13, here are some important observations from this key text that will provide a little hope for you.

- Psalm 13 begins in agitation and ends in calm.
- In Psalm 13, the waves run high at first, but at last lie peacefully glinting in the sunshine.
- In Psalm 13, we find David enduring at first, and then at last we see him singing.

You, too, can be singing when life turns up lemons in your life. Hopefully, Psalm 13 will be an encouragement to you. It is written in order to gently move you forward and help you in making lemonade when life throws lemons your way.

Remember, there are no straight lines in the Bible. Its accounts and stories involve twists and turns (zigzags) that are designed as speed bumps to slow us down, and help us to make better decisions and choices as we travel the roads of life.

Chapter Five Review
Zigzag Realities

Discussion:

Mountains and valleys are those precarious moments where we experience the highs and lows of life. Our positive choices to trust God's loyal love will help us through those challenging times.

1. Paul experienced difficult times in ministry. Does that mean Christians will have tough moments too?
2. God sometimes uses trouble to draw His children closer to Himself. Can you give Scripture to support this truth?
3. Give a testimony demonstrating God's faithfulness in a problem you've encountered. What did you learn from it?
4. Why is Psalm 13 so vitally important to the Christian who is faced with trials and problems?
5. "Negative thinking is a choice." Why is that phrase important?

Goal Setting

What are some goals you would like to achieve as you have read chapter five?

_____

_____

_____

_____

CHAPTER SIX

Zigzag Tips

Years ago, I moved to a little town in Wyoming after I took a semester off from college while I kept my trucking job. That period of time was a strategic opportunity to learn some profitable life lessons for living a happy and successful life.

If we get impetuous and impatient, we may jump into life-changing decisions and choices without giving an iota of thought or prayer to it.

In my case, I sat out a semester from the Bible college I was attending in Billings, Montana. I wasn't happy about my decision, as it set me back a whole semester; but on the other hand, it put me ahead in earning additional funds to add to the money I had already saved up for college.

As another plus, it was a moment of opportunity for me to learn what would later help motivate me to make better choices in my life.

I want to share with you five tips that would eventually springboard me forward into success.

#1: Be Prepared

One of the best ways in moving ahead in life is to be prepared.

Today, it seems like many do not prepare themselves for anything, whether it would be in education, marriage, their occupation, health, or even retirement. Being prepared allows one to live a stress-free life.

When a crisis pops up unannounced, and people are caught off guard, then it's too late! Many hold onto the false notion that they are going to make it to the top with no effort. Not true! I have said it many times: Be prepared! Plan accordingly. If you don't, you'll will find the time down the road of life to be inconvenienced by failure or lloss of goals.

In my younger days, I was one of those individuals who got caught "with my pants down."

I was totally unprepared when, out of the blue, the government sent me a friendly letter telling me I was about to be drafted into the Army. It was 1968, and young men my age who either had quit school, or those who had poor grades, like myself, fit the criteria to be drafted to help fight in the Vietnam War.

Finding myself out of options, I was forced into going down to the military recruiting station where I joined the United States Navy.

I beat the draft by enlisting in the Navy and was successful in enrolling in their 120-day delayed program, which allowed me to finish my high school education. Then just a few weeks after graduating, I was rushed off to an eleven-week basic training program in San Diego, California.

The good news is that God sovereignly had His hands on me. I had just become a new Christian before joining the Navy. That gave me security in knowing God was going to lead me and take care of me. My role was to be faithful in living the Christian life.

"For I know the plans I have for you, says the Lord. They are plans for good and not for evil, to give you a future and a hope" (Jer. 29:11 TLB).

Stuck on an Island

During our last week in boot camp, all of us Navy guys received our orders for where we were being stationed around the world. My military orders assigned me to a Naval Air Base way on the island of Guam. I had no idea where Guam was located, and had to search out its location on a world map. I was stunned to learn it was a tiny island—just thirty miles long and eight miles wide—out in the middle of the Pacific Ocean

Living on base was a new experience for me. Learning how to live on a small, humid, tropical island miles away from friends and family was also a big adjustment. But I knew God was with me, and that He had my best interests in mind, whether my circumstances were good or bad.

John 16:33 (NLT) says, "I have told you all this so that you may have peace in me. Here on earth you will have many trials and sorrows. But take heart, because I have overcome the world."

The second week on the island was worse than the first. I found myself plagued with loneliness. That is when I took it upon myself to do something about my problem.

The second Saturday, my day off, I ventured off base to seek some peace of mind. After walking about a mile or so, I stumbled onto a road sign for the Christian Servicemen's Center with an arrow pointing down a little road.

Curious, I followed that arrow to investigate, and made a great discovery. I found a beautiful building with a breathtaking view overlooking the Pacific Ocean. That servicemen's center became my home away from home. I made instant friends at a place where I could actually think and pray without interruption.

Our director had an amphitheater built in the back of the

center facing the cliff that overlooked the Pacific Ocean. It was grand location for singspirations, plays, and where we military guys could enjoy an outdoor church service.

That amphitheater had another purpose, as I used it as my prayer altar. There in that quiet, private place I could spend quality time in prayer. I would pace those steps and pray for my future life, where I would work, live, and eventually serve the God I loved.

After my tour of duty on Guam, I returned to Treasure Island, California where I received my honorable discharge papers. Everything I had prepared for was being put into place.

I graduated from Bible school, and enrolled in a seminary in Portland, Oregon. At the Christian supply store, I ran into an old friend who eventually introduced me to a beautiful young lady with flaming red hair who later became my wife.

Regardless of our zigzag moments in life, we will need preparation to keep ourselves moving forward, onward, and upward in life. Successful marriages, occupations, and happy lives are not accidents. They take preparation and stick-to-itiveness to pull off. Without preparation, life can become monotonous, confusing, as well as complicated.

One Step at a Time

Back in those military days I paced those amphitheater steps at the Christian Servicemen's Center asking God to give me a special wife.

I later learned that Kathy too was allowing God to prepare herself for me as she rode her horse across the wheat fields her dad had freshly harvested in eastern Washington State.

Kathy's mom and dad allowed her to attend a Word-centered Bible camp where biblical principles of preparation were drilled into the lives of those young people seeking God's best.

At this Bible camp, Kathy ran into a little trouble. She was running across the playfield when she stepped into a hidden hole, and fell to the ground with a seriously twisted ankle.

This unfortunate accident greatly interfered with her plans to finish Bible college. As a result, she was there only for a very brief time. Her ankle was not healing correctly, forcing her to withdraw from the Bible school and return home to the farm.

A short time later, Kathy was able to get around carefully on her foot. She took a job working at her small-town bank. Not long after being employed there, her ankle began acting up again, and she had to take time off from her banking job to allow additional time for it to heal.

After being cooped up a short time at the farmhouse, Kathy's mother wanted to give her a break by taking her to the mall. It was there that an employee from her bank saw her, reported her to the bank manager, and she was terminated shortly after.

Wondering what God was doing with her life, Kathy was asking, *Why is God allowing me all this trouble?*

Her mother encouraged her by saying: "It must all be happening for a reason."

Around this same time, I was attending a liberal arts college in the South where things were not exactly working out for me either. I had spent several thousands of dollars over a period of two years, only to withdraw prematurely without a degree from this institution. I, too, was asking, *Why is this happening to me?*

God was directing Kathy in all her troubles, and He was also directing me through my own painful moments. Our zigzags were sovereignly used in a most divine way to bring Kathy and me together.

Just think, if we had been successful in avoiding all that trouble and had missed those hard times—we would have missed each other.

In both our lives, preparation was part of the process. There has to be preparation. The process is just important as the product. As we do our part, God will do His part in leading His people along the pathways they are to take in life.

"The Lord God is my strength; and he will give me the speed of a deer and bring me safely over the mountains" (Hab. 3:19 TLB).

#2: Pay Attention

One morning Kathy and I took our newborn son for his very first baby checkup. As our pediatrician entered the exam room, I couldn't help notice an instrument that he had pulled out of the pocket of his white jacket. It was a tiny golden bell he used for ear examinations. As soon as he lifted the bell out of his pocket, it made a ringing sound, and Scott's eyes open widely in surprise. It was a precious moment.

The doctor quipped, "Well, at least we know now that this little guy can hear!"

We were totally delighted to see our son reacting to a ringing bell before his examination had even started.

Listening should be as natural and as easily done as the way baby Scott listened to that little bell that morning.

It seems as people age, they somehow lose the ability to listen well—not just hear—but listen. Many people seem to filter what they choose to listen to, and tune out what they do not want to hear. This short circuits valuable information that somehow gets lost or diverted. It's as if information goes in one ear and out the other.

Paying attention is a full-time job. It takes self-discipline and skill to learn to listen well.

One of those skills involves not trying to monopolize the conversation when conversing with others.

Another skill is showing respect by not senselessly interrupting the other person while he or she is trying to communicate a thought. Perhaps that's why God gave people just one mouth to speak and two ears to listen!

In 1 Samuel 3:1–10 (NLT) we read about how the young boy Samuel listened to the voice of God.

> Meanwhile, the boy Samuel served the Lord by assisting Eli. Now in those days messages from the Lord were very rare, and visions were quite uncommon.
>
> One night Eli, who was almost blind by now, had gone to bed. The lamp of God had not yet gone out, and Samuel was sleeping in the Tabernacle near the Ark of God. Suddenly the Lord called out, "Samuel!"
>
> "Yes?" Samuel replied. "What is it?" He got up and ran to Eli. "Here I am. Did you call me?"
>
> "I didn't call you," Eli replied. "Go back to bed." So he did.
>
> Then the Lord called out again, "Samuel!"
>
> Again Samuel got up and went to Eli. "Here I am. Did you call me?"
>
> "I didn't call you, my son," Eli said. "Go back to bed."
>
> Samuel did not yet know the Lord because he had never had a message from the Lord before. So the Lord called a third time, and once more Samuel got up and went to Eli. "Here I am. Did you call me?"
>
> Then Eli realized it was the Lord who was calling the boy. So he said to Samuel, "Go and lie down again, and if someone calls again, say, 'Speak, Lord, your servant is listening.'" So Samuel went back to bed.
>
> And the Lord came and called as before, "Samuel! Samuel!"
>
> And Samuel replied, "Speak, your servant is listening."

#3: Read the Signs

Back in the mid-seventies, I was driving a semi-truck through a little town just outside of Billings when a state patrolman in a Montana State police cruiser pulled me over for speeding.

At the entrance of this little town, there was a sign that read: "Our Town is Like Heaven to Us, Please Do Not Drive Like Hell Through It." My mind must have been on something else, because I was caught speeding.

When the patrolman approached my truck, he wasted no time in asking, "Why were you speeding?"

I repeatedly apologized to him, but he was determined to write me a ticket.

I watched him pull his little citation book from his back pocket as he asked for my commercial driver's license and my medical card. As he was beginning to write me a ticket, he lectured: "You are a truck driver, and part of your job as a professional driver is to read all the signs that are posted along these highways."

No sooner had he said those words, a teenager in a flaming-red hot rod peeled out of the intersection just several feet from where this officer was writing me a ticket.

The state cop quickly returned my driver's license to me and said, "Slow down and be careful!" Then he ran to his patrol car and chased down the teenager.

I was not only a blessed truck driver that morning, but I learned a valuable lesson in paying better attention to all the posted signs.

Part of the zigzag regrets that people fall into in life are from failing to read the signs that are clearly marked out.

Failing to Read the Signs

Most of the married couples with failing relationships I have counseled over the years have failed to read the signs that were visible right in front of them.

I arrived at one home where a broken man was trying to explain to me, as his voice cracked with emotion, why his wife walked out on him. In talking with him, it was evident to me that he missed all the signs his wife was trying to convey.

In another case, a bus driver paged me one day begging me to come and help him. His wife had left a note telling him she was fed up with his abuse and neglect and she was leaving him.

By the time I reached his home, he was in tears, begging me to go and persuade his wife to return home.

Arriving at the mall where she worked, I noticed an overweight security guard dressed in a wrinkled uniform who was approaching her information desk with a cup of coffee and cookie. I noticed that she seemed to be inviting him to come close, and allowed him to hug her and kiss her before he walked away.

I stood there trying to process what I had seen. This security guard was not a handsome guy, nor was he well groomed. He was just a security guard who knew how to romance this attractive and petite blond.

Getting my courage up, I made my way over to her desk and politely introduced myself as the union's chaplain.

As soon as she heard those words, she immediately bristled up, and said, "I'm going to call security if you don't leave immediately."

I returned to the transit driver's house and told him his wife was not returning home. It was extremely hard to tell him she was involved with another man. He dropped to his knees on his living room floor in tears of sorrow.

The sad thing about this whole scenario, is that just months before this episode, I had a conversation with this same bus operator about working unhealthy fifteen hour days and being away from his family and home.

"I know what I'm doing," he told me. "Besides, my wife loves it when I buy her a new car every year."

As I stood in his home with my hand on his shoulder as he sobbed, I thought about how all of this could have been avoided if he would have really listened to his wife. Things could have been different if he only would have taken time to read the signs coming from his now-estranged wife and his heartbroken two little boys.

The apostle Paul said it well in 1 Peter 5:8–9 (ESV): "Be sober-minded; be watchful. Your adversary the devil prowls around like a roaring lion, seeking someone to devour. Resist him, firm in your faith, knowing that the same kinds of suffering are being experienced by your brotherhood throughout the world."

A word to the wise: read the signs!

#4: Remain Courteous

I spent twenty-four years driving for a transit company in the city of Portland. I must admit that I was not the best example in displaying courtesy to the public.

When I first got hired on with the transit district in the summer of 1982, I loved the job at first. However, after a while, the honeymoon experience ended. It was frustrating to me when passengers repeatedly asked the same questions. Over and over again, I'd hear, "Driver, can you tell me the correct time?" Or "Does this bus go downtown?"

I found myself becoming cynical and then rude to them. Some passengers called in, complaining about my job performance and asking the company why they hired rude drivers like me.

One day I boarded several people during the morning rush hour downtown. I always tried to get through town as quickly as possible. As the last person would board at each stop, I would quickly close the front door, trying to get a jackrabbit start and make it through the stoplight before it turned red.

I got so good at this, that I could make it through most of the green lights before they turned red. As I would clear each green light, I could see in my mirror above my head that my riders were hanging on for dear life until they could find a seat.

That particular morning it was raining and cold. I was making my way down the mall loading up passengers and making it through the green lights just like clockwork when I heard a piercing male voice outside yelling at the top of his lungs, "Wait! Wait! Wait!"

But as the last person entered the door, I cavalierly closed it and jackrabbited my way through the intersection just before the light turned red, before making my way down to the next bus stop a block and a half down the mall.

At this next stop, the people boarded quickly as most of them had bus passes, making the process so much easier. Once again, I expeditiously closed the front door and successfully made it through another green light.

Then I heard the same irritating male voice hollering, "Wait! Wait!! Please, wait!!!"

I had almost made it to the end of the mall when the last stoplight turned red. That is when I saw this worn-out looking, middle-aged guy carrying two suitcases huffing up to my front door, totally out of wind.

I remember him placing both his hands on my front doors as if to keep me from closing them. As he gasped for air, he said in between breaths, "Sir, does this bus go to the airport?"

That did it! That was the straw that broke the camel's back for me that morning. At that point I came unglued, and yelled, "Listen up, buddy! Can't you read? There are signs all over this bus saying Airport!"

He looked embarrassed as he dropped his eyes and meekly announced, "Sir, I can't read."

Instantly, I felt like I had been electrocuted. I felt like a jerk! The wind had been taken out of my sails. I wondered how I could redeem myself, but it was obvious the damage had already been done.

At that point, one passenger got up and walked off the bus, glaring at me in disgust. Another passenger got up and pronounced, "You are the most discourteous bus driver of the year."

No matter how hard I tried to apologize, no one wanted to hear a word from me after I had treated the man who couldn't read that way.

In fact, all forty-six bus passengers demonstrated some sort of disapproval of my performance that morning. You could have cut the air with a knife. And I deserved it!

Several days later, I was called in to answer the many complaints that were phoned into the company on my behalf. No matter how hard I tried to explain the incident, the company did not buy it, and informed me to clean up my act.

I walked out of my supervisor's office that day feeling emotionally beat up. As I look back almost thirty-seven years to that dreadful incident, I'm grateful no one on my bus that morning knew anything of my background. They didn't know I was finishing up my last year in seminary and training for the ministry.

In reality, I was a hypocrite. I was a nice student on campus, but a failure in the bus seat. I was totally ashamed of myself!

Hebrews 13:2–3 (NLT) says, "Don't forget to show hospitality to strangers, for some who have done this have entertained angels without realizing it! Remember those in prison, as if you were there yourself. Remember also those being mistreated, as if you felt their pain in your own bodies."

That whole experience was a wake-up call for me. It took a long while to turn that scenario around. From then on, I made it a point to be polite and courteous in dealing with people in public. But it took a couple of years for me to even begin learning how to treat people well in the marketplace.

This was not a class that anyone could take in seminary or at a Bible school. Working for the bus company taught me the best lesson in learning how to get along with people. Imagine, they were paying me the big bucks to do just that.

Several years later while attending a driver's safety awards banquet at the Hilton hotel in downtown Portland, my name was called to come and receive the "Most Outstanding Customer Service Award."

I was totally blown away by receiving this beautiful award! As a result, I was featured on Portland's channel 8 TV program *AM-PM Northwest* as the most outstanding bus operator in the City of Roses.

What I learned reminds me of the admonitions of 2 Tim. 2:3–5 (NLT). "Endure suffering along with me, as a good soldier of Christ Jesus. Soldiers don't get tied up in the affairs of civilian life, for then they cannot please the officer who enlisted them. And athletes cannot win the prize unless they follow the rules."

What Pushes Your Buttons?

What pushes your buttons? Is it impolite or ill-mannered motorist cutting you off in heavy traffic, or someone sitting at a green light while texting? These kinds of senseless acts can be irritating and upsetting.

Today, there seems to be a new normal in the way people drive. For example, I find it most annoying that they will activate their turn signals just as they are making the turn. That simply does not make sense to me at all!

Regardless of what pushes your buttons, the point is, rude people are everywhere. They walk, drive, and behave as if they are the only ones on the planet. These are the same people you see doing some of the craziest things while driving!

I was in rush hour traffic when I witnessed someone typing on his laptop as he moved through heavy traffic. We've all seen women applying makeup while driving, apparently not giving a hoot about anyone around them.

The National Safety Council indicates that driver distractions are the biggest cause of accidents today on our highways and interstates in America. They say people using their cell phones, talking or texting, leads to 1.6 million crashes each year. That results in more than 330,000 injuries caused by uncaring individuals who think of themselves more than the safety of the others around them.

I was walking home from work one early morning after getting off my bus run, when I came upon a car accident that had taken place right out in front of our bus company headquarters. As the tow trucks were removing the cars from the accident scene, I asked the policeman who was writing up his report, "How did this happen?"

The policeman looked at me and sounded disgusted when he said, "He was on his cell phone."

I said, "People need to stop talking on their cell phones while driving."

His response came quickly. "They won't! People will be people."

Profound and true.

Showing common courtesy is a learned behavior. It's the ability to demonstrate kindness, respect, and civility toward others.

I learned the hard way that this needs to begin with me.

Courtesy is to be role-modeled at home, so kids growing up will know how to be kind and have proper boundaries as they move into society, making our world a better place to live.

Deuteronomy 11:19 (NIV) says, "Teach them to your children, talking about them when you sit at home and when you walk along the road, when you lie down and when you get up."

No Service

It was Kathy's birthday, and I was surprising her with a birthday dinner at a very expensive restaurant. As I opened the two huge wooden doors for Kathy, the smell of delicious food was intoxicating—drawing us into what we hoped would be a night of feasting.

But we were surprised to see the lobby empty when we walked in. There was a posted sign reading "Please Wait to Be Seated" so we stood in that lobby for several minutes. Finally, a dishwasher coming through with a cart of dirty dishes asked, "Have you been helped?"

As we looked around, the restaurant didn't seem to be all that busy. A moment or two later, someone other than a hostess or a waitress approached us and tried to be helpful. She had a difficult time locating two menus and finding a table for us.

We patiently waited for someone to approach us to take our order, but no one showed up. That was it! We walked out disgusted. This restaurant was well known by name, yet in our experience, it lacked a proper philosophy of customer service. It didn't seem to have a clue how to serve the public. Kathy and I have never returned to that restaurant again.

Great customer service is something that sells people, or turns people away. People want things explained to them. People want to go to places that spoil them with courtesy, and allow them a special time out.

Philippians 2:4 (ESV) says, "Let each of you look not only to his own interests, but also to the interests of others."

No Welcome

When I was eighteen, over a long period of time, I made it my mission to invite my dad to attend church with me. One Sunday I was ecstatic to see him standing there in the church vestibule unannounced.

As our morning session ended, and everyone was filing out, I noticed all the men walked directly past him without greeting him. I was deeply disturbed that no one took the time to stop and say hello, or find out his name. I was stunned!

My dad walked out and never again returned to that church. When I got home that afternoon, I tried to cover for those irresponsible people who weren't courteous to him.

Later my dad informed me that he was choosing another church—which we would consider a cult—where he not only felt accepted, but where they rolled out the red carpet for him. My dad became a regular attender of that church, as well as a tither.

If we are going to be successful with people in the marketplace and effectively evangelize them, we have to learn to practice more courtesy within the walls of this living organism—the church.

John 13:34–35 (TLB) says, "And so I am giving a new commandment to you now—love each other just as much as I love you. Your strong love for each other will prove to the world that you are my disciples."

A modern paraphrase of the Bible puts these words into 21st century perspective, giving us the big picture in becoming courteous people:

> If you've gotten anything at all out of following Christ, if his love has made any difference in your life, if being in a community of the Spirit means anything to you, if you have a heart, if you *care*— then do me a favor: Agree with each other, love each other, be deep-spirited friends. Don't push your way to the front; don't sweet-talk your way to the top. Put yourself aside, and help others get ahead. Don't be obsessed with getting your own advantage. Forget yourselves long enough to lend a helping hand. (Phil. 2:3–4 MSG)

#5: Practice Patience

Back in 1994, I took on the biggest challenge of my life. I had been accepted in the doctor of ministry program at Western

Seminary in Portland. This challenge not only affected my life, but equally the lives of my family members.

It involved a huge commitment that was to last four long years. It would take money (lots of money), time, and commitment to meet all the demands and deadlines to complete this program. It took patience and perseverance to make it to graduation day, April 16, 1998, a day I will never forget.

After the completion of this intense program, it took almost a full year for me to air myself out and to get my life back to normal.

I could never repay Kathy for her unselfish dedication in holding our family together by caring for our two children, keeping all the bills current, and making sure our home was in order.

I was simply up to my neck in educational responsibility and fulfilling my role as a transit operator working forty hours a week, plus carrying out my chaplain's role in counseling and caring for our employees who kept the transportation wheels rolling along in the city of Portland.

Kathy and I learned to stay a step ahead of our educational goals without getting distracted by anger or irritation with one another. We learned a lot through the process of practicing patience.

Perhaps you are going through your own difficult wilderness of trouble that tries to tie you down. You may feel as if you can't see the light at the end of the tunnel.

My sister-in-law, Naomi, is facing this challenge. Her husband, Dan was diagnosed with multiple sclerosis several years ago. He lost full use of his legs and is now in a wheelchair. Naomi patiently waits on Dan, and there seems to be no end to her loving service in caring for him.

Regardless of your challenges in life, I would encourage you to hang in there. God will make a way when there seems to be no way. One positive thing that flows from these hardships is they keep us on our knees in prayer.

Joshua in the Old Testament was a man who had his own challenges and delays in following God. His affirming words to the Israelites can bring us profound comfort in our challenges.

> Be strong and brave, for you will be a successful leader of my people; and they shall conquer all the land I promised to their ancestors. You need only to be strong and courageous and to obey to the letter every law Moses gave you, for if you are careful to obey every one of them, you will be successful in everything you do. (Joshua 1:6–7 TLB)

Chapter Six Review
Zigzag Tips

Discussion:

To make your life a little easier on Planet Earth, make the most out of the zigzags of your life.

1. Name the five tips in this chapter that will help navigate through the zigzags of life.
2. Which tip is one that you personally need to work on?
3. Discuss why John 16:33 is so important for the believer.
4. List a tip in this chapter that has helped you in dealing with people.
5. The doctorate program shaped my life. How has working through challenging circumstances shaped your life?

Goal Setting

What are some goals you would like to achieve as you have read chapter six?

CHAPTER SEVEN

Precarious Curves

I n our US road systems, there are many reasons for the unpredictable curves we encounter. One of the biggest reasons is because of lakes, mountains, or huge buildings—those unmovable obstacles that seem to interfere with the road's intended straight-line direction.

Even though some of those dubious curves can become a nuisance at times, they can help keep drivers safe and alert.

A good example is Interstate 94 that crosses North Dakota.

Back in the summer of 1974, I took a job with a ma and pa trucking company out of Park River, North Dakota, called Larson & Sons. They hired me right out of Bible school as one of their truck drivers to transport their North Dakota red potatoes to market.

One of the many trucking routes I would take was I-94 that led from Fargo, North Dakota to Glendive, Montana. I remember how difficult it was to make that five-and-a-half-hour run across the state of North Dakota (389 miles) through the middle of the night.

I witnessed unusual truck and car accidents on every trip across that stretch of interstate, it seemed. There was no other reason to explain some of those accidents other than drivers getting bored and falling asleep at the wheel. Unusual for me, I found it very difficult to stay awake myself. I'd fight off heavy eyes and fatigue, trying to keep that straight highway from hypnotizing me.

Curves and hills on the road became a welcomed sight. They'd keep us drivers focused until we were able to make it to the truck stop in Glendive, where we could take a break, get some hot coffee and something to eat.

Dangerous curves are usually announced ahead of time by bright yellow, diamond-shaped road signs with a big black curved arrow. Those signs usually accompany a posted speed sign helping drivers execute a safe speed throughout the turn, and potentially preventing an accident.

The Caution Signs of Life

In life, it works the same way. But instead of posted signs and warnings, verbal warnings from others to take caution will keep us out of trouble.

When I was eleven years old, I began bumping up against some of those caution signs.

My dad took a job as a newspaperman in Pasco, a little town in central Washington State. Back in the late fifties and early sixties, Pasco was a very small town out in the middle of the desert. There was really nothing there. It was kind of a quiet, sleepy little town adjoined with two other little towns across the Snake River, one called Kennewick, and Richland, a few miles west. These three little towns collectively were better known as the Tri-Cities.

My dad was employed by the Columbia Basin Newspaper Company in Pasco. After living in Pasco for a couple of years, I became a newspaper delivery boy, delivering newspapers early in the mornings, long before the sun would pop up.

We lived in the Project, better known as the Navy Homes Project. The Project involved a lot of buildings that were used to house Navy personnel and their families during World War II. These one-to-three-bedroom apartments were adjoined with three or four other attached apartments, together making up one long building.

Since there were many of these buildings closely located together, no one had a backyard. All the front yards were small, so there was no place for kids my age to play. However, the Project did have a spacious, beautifully-manicured baseball diamond just about a block from where our family lived. And that's where I fell in love with playing baseball.

I found myself playing along with a gang of other little boys my age who gathered every day before the sun rose to play ball. We played until our mothers called us home for dinner, and after dinner, until it was difficult to see our hands after the sun went down.

No one worried about being abducted. These were innocent years, filled with love and excitement for the game.

There was this older kid who was kind of our leader, as well as our pitcher. And he knew how to throw a fast curve ball. He knew how to intimidate and scare anyone who was up to bat as he was totally unpredictable. You just didn't know what the guy was going to throw your way.

I'm not sure why, but when it was my turn to step up to the plate, this pitcher seemed to have it in for me. In fact, his body language strongly indicated to me that he was out to make my experience a bad one.

The problem is, he was successful! He simply had the ability to throw such a curve ball that it would literally whiz by my face. It didn't take long for him to strike me out every time I got up to bat.

Connecting at Last

About a year into playing this game every day, I began adjusting to this pitcher's intimidating body language and mean-spirited curveballs, which were his signature pitch in striking out so many little kids my age.

Time went on. I kept trying and others encouraged me not to give up. My self-confidence grew day by day and I became a better batter.

Then one day it happened. I actually connected with one of his evil hardballs. It flew so high and so far that it eventually went over the fence line. I had hit a home run! It was one of the happiest days of my life. I was so overjoyed I peed my pants.

For the first time ever, I felt totally successful, like I had accomplished some major obstacle. That particular day, the cracking of the bat when the hardball was hurled into space became my "wow" moment in life! I'm almost certain that my mom heard my scream of joy all the way to my house as I yelled, "YAAAHOOOO!" I felt totally triumphant.

The very next time up to bat, I slammed another home run. Then another one after that one. I soon captured a reputation as one of the best batters in my neighborhood.

I knew things had turned around when that pitcher came up to me and said, "Tommy, you have done a good job in learning how to become a great batter. I only threw those unpredictable curveballs your way to help you become the player you are today. Way to go!"

Those words meant so very much to me. They were affirming and healing and helped me in becoming the spiritual man I have become today. That pitcher helped me move to the next level by encouraging me to take control of my life. The encouragement from my friends also helped my self-esteem take a big jump on that special day.

Since then I have often thanked God for difficult and challenging "pitchers" who have thrown dastardly balls my direction.

I often remind others that life is not fair. Risky curves exist for our benefit, and they must be dealt with if we are to move onward, forward, and upward in life. I encourage others to not give up at their first terrorizing curve.

My message is simple: Stay with it. Pursue excellence. There will always be obstacles to face. Curves exist for our benefit. It takes dogged perseverance, iron discipline, and hard work to adjust to those curves. Zero in and don't allow anything to distract you from the direction you are trying go. Remember: If you aim at nothing you will hit it. Just keep pressing forward with all the torque and horsepower you can muster up.

In trucking, horsepower and torque are everything. Horsepower is the ability to maintain the speed you have achieved, while torque is the ability to accelerate and pull. This is important when it comes to zigging vs. zagging through the dangerous curves of life you will be facing.

Keep Pedaling

I taught this principle to my daughter Pamela when she was just four years old. I had bought her a bicycle with training wheels so she could comfortably and safely enjoy pedaling her way safely down the sidewalk. After a time, she asked me to remove those training wheels. I tried talking her out of it, but she insisted. She wanted the freedom to ride using her own balance.

She was (still is!) a persistent little girl, so I took off the training wheels. I also told her, "Balancing on your own is something you'll have to learn. The secret is to keep pedaling." I knew it was her horsepower and torque that would keep her from falling over.

The day I took her training wheels off, I ran alongside her saying, "Keep pedaling!" Finally that magic moment appeared.

Pamela was doing everything I taught her—she was pedaling and balancing!

With a lot of faith, I finally let her go. I held my breath as I watched her intently concentrate on keeping her balance. She was so careful and graceful too! I kept yelling: "Pamela, keep pedaling! Don't stop! Keep pedaling." Sure enough, she was doing it!

The only problem was, I forgot to teach her how to stop. I began chasing after her, slowly catching up to her, and brought her to a safe stop. Then I gave her the biggest hug!

Pamela, who today is a successful CPA, happily married, with a handsome little boy and a new baby girl, learned the principle of pedaling hard early on in life.

All of us can utilize this same principle. All we need to do is just begin to pedal, balance, and stay with it. We can do this!

Are you zigging or are you zagging through those precarious curves in your life? Here are some good questions to ask yourself to find out.

- Do you make sound decisions?
- Are you frustrated with your present circumstances?
- Do you feel restless, feeling left out in life?
- Are you depressed—feeling inadequate?
- Are you lacking energy and living off your memories?

If you said yes to any of the above questions, then you are zagging. If this describes your present circumstances, then do something about it. Resolve in your mind that you will act and move out from under your fears.

On November 12th, 2012, our world lost the positive voice of a man who was a champion in helping those stuck in life—Zig Ziglar. Ziglar addressed this specific issue when he said:

The first step in solving any problem or meeting any challenge is to be sure it is properly identified. Negative thinking is when you throw up your hands in despair and say, "I've never been able to do this before. This is a hopeless situation, or there's nothing I can do." The picture these words paint in your mind will stifle your creative imagination and create an even bigger problem than the one that already exists.[2]

The apostle Paul echoes almost the same message of hope when he penned these positive words in AD 61: "And now, brothers, as I close this letter, let me say this one more thing: Fix your thoughts on what is true and good and right. Think about things that are pure and lovely, and dwell on the fine, good things in others. Think about all you can praise God for and be glad about" (Phil. 4:8 TLB).

Possessing a positive attitude makes a difference in our lives.

Years ago, I won an award at the bus company where I was employed. I had received a good number of commendations from many who rode my bus. As a result, one of the managers came out to where I was driving bus, boarded the bus at a stop, and announced to all my passengers that I had won an award.

One of the gifts that was presented to me was a cap with a very interesting message on it. It read "Attitudes Are the Real Disabilities."

When we allow negative attitudes to interfere with our performance, the end result will be failure and disappointment.

I find this to be true in officiating funerals. I've noticed a big difference in working with families who are spiritually in tune with God and attend church, versus those who do not.

It's all in how we think and live. The apostle Paul lived out this example. God had sovereignly placed him as a prisoner in

---

[2] Zig Ziglar, *Over the Top* (Chicago: Thomas Nelson Publishers, 1994), 115–117.

the prison system of Rome around AD 58. Writing from prison, he expressed the following everlasting truth, as the Spirit of God directed him:

> With eyes wide open to the mercies of God, I beg you, my brothers, as an act of intelligent worship, to give him your bodies, as a living sacrifice, consecrated to him and acceptable by him. Don't let the world around you squeeze you into its own mould, but let God re-mould your minds from within, so that you may prove in practice that the plan of God for you is good, meets all his demands and moves towards the goal of true maturity. (Rom. 12:1–2 Phillips)

Another paraphrase sheds additional light on this same particular passage of Scripture. Notice the language as expressed in 21st century language.

> So here's what I want you to do, God helping you: Take your everyday, ordinary life—your sleeping, eating, going-to-work, and walking-around life—and place it before God as an offering. Embracing what God does for you is the best thing you can do for him. Don't become so well-adjusted to your culture that you fit into it without even thinking. Instead, fix your attention on God. You'll be changed from the inside out. Readily recognize what he wants from you, and quickly respond to it. Unlike the culture around you, always dragging you down to its level of immaturity, God brings the best out of you, develops well-formed maturity in you. (Rom. 12:1–2 MSG)

Paul's message to the church in Rome is simple: Stop letting society change you. Paul points out an important truth: A genuine Christian has the benefit of being Spirit directed.

If I was going to give this strategic passage of Scripture in Romans 12:1–2 a title, it would be "Mastering the Master Plan." God has a master plan for us to follow, even though the road of life will twist and turn. We must be alert and watchful as we travel down those uncertain roads, but God will direct us.

The subject of this amazing text is the will of God. Paul wants the Roman Christians to know they can know the will of God on the road of life. This passage could also be titled, "God's Blueprint for Christian Living." God has a plan for His people that will provide safety and direction on the roads of life.

It's important to know God's purposes for our daily lives as we travel the road of life with all its uncertain curves. How can we know for sure we can stay safe on precarious roads with all their twists and turns? How is that possible, especially when we live in an uncertain world?

Romans 12:1–2 tells us we are to be Spirit-driven individuals. Having a purpose in life and being Spirit-driven makes the road of life interesting and fun.

How do we become Spirit-driven?

The answer lies in this Bible text: Romans 12:1–2. Let's dig a little deeper to learn some crystal-clear steps for staying safe in those zigzags and curves of life.

Step #1: You Must Be Saved (Rom. 12:1)

People need to know if they are really saved and members of God's family or not. In Romans 12:1 (NIV) Paul says, "Therefore, I urge you, brothers, in view of God's mercy, to offer your bodies as living sacrifices, holy and pleasing to God—this is your spiritual act of worship." What exactly is Paul speaking about here?

He is speaking about being a genuine Christian—the real deal!

Let me tell you about an experience that happened to me back in my Navy days. I was on my way to Baguio, Philippines from Guam in order to attend a Christian Servicemen's conference.

As our plane approached the Baguio airfield, there were a good number of people loitering on the runway. Our Air Force pilot radioed the control tower asking them to make an announcement to get the people off the airfield so we could land.

After our plane finally touched down and came to a stop, I was the first one off the plane. As I stepped onto the pavement, I saw a couple of guys who were on their knees digging into the tarmac. I asked, "What in the world are you digging?"

"We're digging out pieces of gold," one man said. There was a gold mine on the other side of the runway, and as the big trucks would cross over, gold would spill off the trucks onto the runway, crushing it into the hot tarmac.

"You'd better call security," I said.

One man looked at me and obnoxiously said, "Who do you think we are?" Then one of them dug out three small chunks of gold and gave them to me.

I kept those three chunks of gold for fifty-two years thinking I had the read deal. Then one day I wanted to take my wife on a special date, and decided it was time to sell that gold.

I walked into a store that handled gold and proudly turned over my loot to the clerk in hopes of exchanging it for money. A couple of minutes later, the clerk informed me that those three chunks of gold were fool's gold, which had no value whatsoever.

Here I had been walking around for all those years thinking I had something of value, when in fact, I had nothing. It was all imitation—not the real deal. That was such a disappointment.

Scripture warns of another kind of imitation, when it says, "Check up on yourselves. Are you really Christians? Do you pass the test? Do you feel Christ's presence and power more and more within you? Or are you just pretending to be Christians when actually you aren't at all?" (2 Cor. 13:5 TLB).

Paul is speaking in this Bible text about being the real deal—

being a genuine Christian. This can be described in a Greek word dakimazo, meaning "to examine."

In other words, we are to prove, test, and scrutinize to examine whether we are real Christians or just impostors. This examination will certify that someone is not being deceived or tricking themselves—and duping others.

Here's the bottom line: Going to church doesn't make one a Christian any more than sleeping in a garage makes them a car.

Each one of us needs to know if we are the real McCoy, truly a bona fide child of the living God.

Notice Paul isn't addressing his comments to the world. In Romans 12:1 he uses a noun that clearly describes a certain class of people. He says, "Therefore, I urge you brethren . . ." Using the word "brethren" proves he is speaking directly to Christians and not to anyone else.

Paul is offering an opportunity for people to examine themselves, ensuring they are truly authentic believers.

Paul's point is crystal clear: salvation is through Jesus Christ alone. It's not through our own efforts to earn our way into heaven. Salvation comes directly from Jesus and is His gift to mankind.

Ephesians 2:8–9 (NIV) says, "For it is by grace you have been saved, through faith—and this is not from yourselves, it is the gift of God—not by works, so that no one can boast." Acts 4:12 (NCV) says, "Jesus is the only One who can save people. No one else in the world is able to save us."

If you are uncertain of your standing in Jesus Christ, I invite you to pray this prayer.

> *Dear Jesus*, I want to be a genuine Christian serving You. I want to be in heaven with You one day. I'm tired of living in the flesh, pleasing only myself. Today I want to place my total trust in You. I'm inviting You into my

life as my Lord and Savior. I give You the title deed of my life. Please forgive all my sins. I want to serve You the rest of my life, living for You moment by moment, depending on Your grace to lead me. Help me to grow in Your grace and love. Thank you for this new life. I surrender all to You. In Jesus' name, amen.

If this is your prayer, you have just made an incredible decision today to follow Jesus Christ. Congratulations! You have just been born into the family of God. "But to all who did receive him, who believed in his name, he gave the right to become children of God, who were born, not of blood nor of the will of the flesh nor of the will of man, but of God" (John 1:12–13 esv).

This is the beginning step in understanding God's will for your life—and it's certainly a beginning in being a Spirit-directed Christian.

Step #2: You Must Be Surrendered (Rom. 12:1b)

The second key to staying safe in the precarious curves of life is to develop a surrendered spirit. Ask yourself at this very moment, "Am I surrendered to God?"

If you look closely at the wording in Romans 12:1, Paul zeros in on a specific truth when he writes: ". . . offer your bodies as a living sacrifice, holy and pleasing to God."

As we see in the context of Romans 12, Paul is driving home the biblical truth that if one is genuine, then there is an element of being surrendered that accompanies it.

The word surrendered has a profound meaning: "not expecting anything in return." This doesn't imply that if I do something as positive as surrendering my will, that I'm going to get something really big out of it from God. On the contrary, yielding our lives to the Lord simply means we are giving up our rights to Him so He can use us as clean, living vessels for His glory.

Many of us like to sing that old hymn of the faith, "I Surrender All." Written by Judson W. Van DeVenter in 1896, the words say, "All to Jesus I surrender, all to Him I freely give, I will ever love and trust Him, in His presence daily live. I surrender all, I surrender all, all to Thee my blessed Savior, I surrender all."

These powerful and touching words are often sung by someone who wants to be in step with the Savior. Anyone can sing the heartfelt words of this beautiful hymn when everything is going well and money is in the bank. However, if we are out of fellowship, and are not surrendering to Christ on a daily basis, it's easy to just sing the hymn without really meaning the words we are singing.

Consider the words of the hymn written by Frances R. Havergal back in 1874 that say, "Take my life and let it be consecrated, Lord, to Thee. Take my moments and my days, let them flow in endless praise."

Surrendering takes personal responsibility to spend time daily with Christ, and actively allow the Holy Spirit to lead and direct our lives moment by moment, regardless of our circumstances.

The apostle Paul writes: "But I say, walk by the Spirit, and you will not gratify the desires of the flesh" (Gal. 5:16 esv). Paul is helping Christians understand that there are many distractions in life (much like construction zones) that will cause us to get out of step with God. We need to keep our minds and lives focused, and walk in dependence upon the Spirit of the living God.

Jude weighs in on this thought when he uses the imperative (a command) as he implores believers by these words: "Stay always within the boundaries where God's love can reach and bless you. Wait patiently for the eternal life that our Lord Jesus Christ in his mercy is going to give you" (Jude 21 TLB).

God wants *all* of us! Not just part of us, or just on Sundays. In God's love letter (the Bible), He provides road signs enabling believers. Christ is in the business of directing us through His written revelation—the Bible. He gives us the Holy Spirit to direct us and depend upon.

Being surrendered is a stepping stone on the pathways through all the precarious construction zones of life. Born again believers who follow in the footsteps of Jesus are Spirit directed.

Step #3: You Must Be Separated (Rom. 12:2a)

In Daniel 1:3–8 we see King Nebuchadnezzar was trying to change Daniel to become more Babylonian than Hebrew. Just the same way, Satan and his evil followers are seriously trying to influence and change the Christian.

Michael Green in his book, *I Believe in Satan's Downfall,* wrote:

> The tempter seeks to embroil men in the same alienation from God which he has willingly chosen for himself. . . . It means a society which leaves God out of account. . . .
>
> We are all placed in situations where we are influenced by other people. That influence, particularly the power of the peer group, the gang, the work mates, the boardroom, the media, is very strong.[3]

Satan, through the world's systems, tries to brainwash Christians into thinking that living for God is old-fashioned and out of style—and a waste of time in the 21st century. Satan tries to lure believers to disengage from following Christ Jesus by making the Bible (God's love letter to the world) seem to be an old, irrelevant book filled with myths, lies, and errors.

The world eagerly sends its false messages loud and clear to anyone who has ears to hear. We hear clever slogans like: "Everyone Is Doing It; Come on! Let it All Hang Out; Do Your Thing; Question Authority." These memorable phrases continue to try to lure and influence anyone with their slippery tentacles.

---

[3] Michael Green, *I Believe in Satan's Downfall* (Grand Rapids, MI: William B. Eerdmans Pub. Co., 1981), 44, 53.

But the Scripture says, "Do not love the world or the things in the world. If anyone loves the world, the love of the Father is not in him. For all that is in the world—the desires of the flesh and the desires of the eyes and pride of life—is not from the Father but is from the world" (1 John 2:15–16 ESV).

Step #4: Be Spiritually Minded (Rom. 12:2)

The last characteristic is found in Romans 12:2 (NIV). "Do not conform any longer to the pattern of this world, but be transformed by the renewing of your mind." This involves the way we choose to use our minds, enabling us to live differently in a pagan society.

Living differently involves thinking differently. It's much like a computer. You put garbage in, you will get garbage out. Your computer does what you program it to do. Our minds work the same way.

I'm convinced the only possible way to keep the world's systems from getting a firm grip on our minds is by having renewed minds. We have to think differently in order to avoid those unwanted solicitations to evil.

While in Kenya on a ministry trip recently, Kathy and I visited the crocodile park just outside of Nairobi. There we saw many crocodiles shaped into something that looked like dry stones. But while they looked like dry stone, they were alive and real, with open mouths and sharp teeth. They appeared to be just patiently waiting for something to pass by so they could snatch onto their next meal.

The enormous size of the crocodiles was almost hypnotizing as we stared at them. I found myself not being able to take my eyes off them. When the park employee took a large branch with a big cloth attached to the end of it and waved it near their heads, they surprised us by quickly coming alert and trying to snatch the cloth.

The man said, "If someone would jump the fence and go inside, without a doubt, he would never return." That was a sobering thought that made me thankful not to be living near these ferocious creatures.

This is the whole argument in Romans 12:2 when it says, "Do not be conformed to this world, but be transformed by the renewing of your mind." Paul is warning us not to jump the fence in trying to walk through this evil corrupt world. The lure of sin can be like the bright and inviting lights of Broadway. Innocent victims are drawn into the web of sin only to be devoured one bite at a time.

Having a renewed mind makes it possible to escape danger. The word transformed found in verse 2 is the Greek word *metamorph*. This particular word is from where we get our English word "metamorphosis." It simply means to undergo a complete change of one's mind under the transforming power of God. God can free our sluggish way of living, thinking, and behaving and give us a fresh purpose in living a Christian life, and glorifying God's name.

While attending seminary back in the late seventies, I owned a beautiful hot rod. My 1971 Ford Grand Torino was a metallic Acapulco blue. It was a super-cool-looking ride with traction bars and wide tires. I even had the engine souped-up with an exhaust system that made her growl when peeling out.

One day my ride began acting sluggish and dull, as if it was mechanically constipated. It was backfiring and running rough. It simply was not a fun car to drive that particular day. It wasn't until I had it mechanically looked at and fixed that she ran like a dream again. All she needed was a simple tune-up to correct the problem.

A Spiritual Tune-Up

Having our minds renewed is the same idea. A renewal is a spiritual tune-up that takes place to make our spiritual life come

118

alive. Christ is in the business of renewing the believer.

There is no other substitute that can accomplish this transformational miracle that the apostle Paul is talking about. It's a beautiful picture of that metamorphosis—that biological change—that happens when a caterpillar turns into a beautiful butterfly. Christ offers a new beginning.

Those who negligently and carelessly take their lives into their own hands by doing whatever feels good without following God's guidelines are asking for trouble. It's like walking into a crocodile pit.

There is a true story about some Englishmen who learned this truth the hard way. They were in a foreign land, and being hungry, they ate a plant, not being aware of its poisonous properties. The plant gave off a false sensation that caused them to lose their hunger pains. But within a short period of time, they all died, one by one.

Spiritual malnutrition has the same negative effect on believers. Without a renewed mind, there will be consequences.

Satan is real; he's a deceiver, an impostor who gives false hope and empty promises. He's a liar, deceiving those who are open to his tricks and schemes. He can make bad things look safe and good like those crocodiles who patiently lie so still waiting for their next bite of food.

This is why being in fellowship with the Lord, being involved in a local church, and spending time in the Word of God, are so vitally important. They will affect the way we think, act, live, and worship.

These two verses that open up Romans 12 give hope and assurance that the believer can choose to be a transformed Christian. Being genuinely saved, surrendered, separated, and spiritually minded is how to live as a Spirit-driven individual in a pagan world.

Remember, precarious curves are your friends. Don't fight them—embrace them! They are blessings in disguise. Their sole purpose for existing is to slow people down and purposely get them out of the fast lane of life.

"But to all who believed him and accepted him, he gave the right to become children of God. They are reborn—not with a physical birth resulting from human passion or plan, but a birth that comes from God" (John 1:12–13 NLT).

"But even though we were dead in our sins God, who is rich in mercy, because of the great love he had for us, gave us life together with Christ—it is, remember, by grace and not by achievement that you are saved—and has lifted us right out of the old life to take our place with him in Christ in the Heavens" (Eph. 2:4–5 Phillips).

Chapter Seven Review
Precarious Curves

Discussion

Precarious curves not only exist in our highway system, but also in our lives. Don't give up when things get tough and difficult to manage.

1. Name some of the lessons baseball taught me.
2. Have you encountered "fools' gold" in your life experiences?
3. Why is Romans 12:1–2 so important for the Christian?
4. List the four steps that start with S in Romans 12:1–2.
5. How have you experienced the world trying to change you into conforming to its ways?

Goal Setting

What are some goals you would like to achieve as you have read chapter seven?

CHAPTER EIGHT

First Things First

Each Saturday morning when I wake up, I ask Kathy, "Do we have a plan for the day?" Plans are important. Without them, there's no direction, no order, or purpose.

When making plans, it's a wise thing to do first things first.

Before a pilot takes a flight, he first takes the necessary steps. He checks the weather. Then he files a flight plan. Filing a flight plan is just basic common sense, as well as a regulation. It gives a pilot assurance of separation from other aircraft he may encounter in or around his airspace.

Maybe it would be nice if ordinary people could file for something like a "people plan" to keep from running into one another in the rat race of life.

Just several days ago, I went shopping at a busy shopping mall. I wasn't in the store for more than five minutes before a young man in his mid-twenties ran directly into me while he was texting. I looked him in the eyes and quipped, "Dude, you need a plan when walking into a busy department store. Now put away your phone!" He looked shocked and did not respond.

Unprepared

On weekends in the Northwest, hundreds of young people hike the mountain trails to experience the gorgeous panoramic views. During one cold fall weekend in 2014, two friends spontaneously decided to go hiking on Mt. Hood.

While not novice hikers, they failed to notice the ominous weather warning reports that had popped up at the last minute. They did not take a tracking device that would enable rescuers to locate them in case something went wrong.

Several hours into the hike, the weather turned treacherous, forcing them to turn back. They didn't make it. Their bodies were not discovered until the following spring. The hike turned into a heartbreaking story that aired on the evening news.

You can probably think of other accounts where family, friends, or loved ones have impetuously disregarded a "flight plan," made foolish decisions and choices, and experienced unfavorable outcomes as a result.

There are four practical characteristics to watch for in those unpredictable zigzag moments. I call these characteristics the Four Ds.

D #1: Distractions

People today seem to be more easily distracted than ever before. What distracts you? Cell phones, long grocery lines, or noisy neighbors?

When I drive down any interstate or road system in America, it's common for me to see distracted individuals with some electronic device in their hands or in their laps. This is not only dangerous, but totally against the law in most states.

There is nothing more unsafe and discourteous than seeing someone at a stoplight totally preoccupied in texting while others sit patiently behind them waiting for them to move through the intersection on a green light.

It's not just cell phones that can be distracting, but how about the ones who primp and apply makeup while driving to work, or others who eat and drive. These are just a few of the senseless distractions that can be annoying and dangerous.

Recently, I spotted a guy with his laptop placed between his belly and steering wheel, carelessly typing away while weaving in and out of traffic on a busy interstate. He must have had a serious report to finish for a business meeting he was running late to attend that morning!

Being distracted is serious business, and it needs to stop. Distractions cause people to fix their eyes on inappropriate things, which causes them to deviate from the course they are following.

I'm not sure if there is a remedy or a plan for all the distractions on the highways of America. Perhaps the answer is the self-driving cars that automobile manufacturers are putting on the market.

Self-driving cars do not apply makeup, they do not drink or eat while they are in driving mode, and don't get distracted. They do what they are designed to do, and nothing more.

Back in my Navy days, I was emptying a pallet of old and obsolete Navy records that were no longer needed by my department. As I was standing on top of a huge dumpster emptying boxes of garbage, a Navy pickup surprised me by recklessly speeding around the corner of my building, its tires squealing.

As soon as the driver spotted me on top of this huge dumpster, he immediately began showing off by honking and swerving his pickup back and forth, waving his hand to capture my attention.

He was obviously out of control when he carelessly drove past me. And when he plowed into an empty forty-foot parked semi-truck it made a loud crashing sound I shall never forget.

Fortunately, he wasn't hurt, but the Navy pickup was

demolished. A couple of days after the Navy investigated his accident, the sailor was cited with negligent driving.

We all have a choice to keep ourselves from being distracted by those things that will harm us and others. Focusing our attention on inappropriate things only leads to regrets.

Keeping first things first will help us fix our eyes on where we need to be going. The Greek word for "goal" is *skopew* meaning "to fix one's eyes on." This is something to aim for in navigating those zigzags of life.

We need to be responsible for our actions and what we do. It's called being obedient.

Follow the Instructions

A businessman left instructions for his staff before leaving on a business trip. He said, "Sell, sell, sell the product while I'm away." He added, "This will make my day and show how responsible you are."

During his absence, the staff members held a meeting and decided to surprise their boss with a freshly painted and redecorated office. They drifted away from the instructions their boss had given.

Upon their boss's return, he walked into the office surprised to find a new paint job and new office furniture.

When the employees began showing up for work, they told the boss, "Look how responsible we've been while you were gone. And we fixed up the office!"

But the boss just asked them, "Did you follow my instructions?"

The staff members could brag all they wanted about how hard they worked in getting the office fixed up, making their workspace comfortable and practical to everyone's satisfaction. They could talk about the new carpet, paint scheme, and new office furniture. But the boss evaluated these well-intentioned employees on their obedience and faithfulness in following through on his instructions. He held them accountable.

Remember the words of Philippians 3:13–14 (TLB): "No, dear brothers, I am still not all I should be, but I am bringing all my energies to bear on this one thing: Forgetting the past and looking forward to what lies ahead, I strain to reach the end of the race and receive the prize for which God is calling us up to heaven because of what Christ Jesus did for us."

D #2: Directionless

Without direction, we're lost in the woods without a compass. Having direction will keep us out of the "hot seat" of unfavorable circumstances.

First things first must be practiced if we want to experience success. First things first involves thinking rightly—not missing the mark.

If you desire a happy home with children, you first must find a good wife, and live together in harmony and love. That gives direction to your goal—producing a happy family. If you aim at nothing, you will hit it.

People without direction are prone to take shortcuts in life, by dating the wrong people, or avoiding marriage altogether, even if they want a happy home with children. A lack of a rational goal and proper direction only leads to disappointment and frustration.

If you want to become a medical doctor and you don't want to attend medical school or study, your goal of becoming a doctor will be short-circuited.

Getting entangled into these kinds of zigzag situations only leads to disappointment and regret. First things first must take place if you want to move ahead to achieve your heart's desire.

Start Planning

Back in college I read *If You Don't Know Where You Are Going, You'll Probably End Up Somewhere Else* by David Campbell. This book put the principle of having direction into proper perspective for me and helped me think about where I needed to be going in life. Its message is still so important I've decided to include it here for your benefit.

Campbell writes about interviewing a successful businessman named Charlie about his career, asking him, "What led to your success?"

Charlie answered: "A lot of luck, but a lot of planning, too."

Then Campbell asked, "When did you start planning?"

"I can tell you exactly when because I remember it as if it were yesterday."

Then Charlie told this story:

> I was in college, living in the dormitory with a boy from Iowa. He came in one night while a bunch of us guys were sitting around talking. I could tell he was excited, but he didn't say anything until everyone else left. Then he blurted, "My folks just got rich! My mother called tonight—she walked out to the mailbox this morning and found a check for $89,000." My reaction, after the initial astonishment, was only barely concealed envy. I asked him what it was all about.
>
> He said, "I don't know exactly everything, but I guess my dad bought some stock back in the depression and then forgot all about it. The company has just been sold, and this is his share."
>
> That night I lay in bed awake a long time, thinking. Why was it his family and not mine? Why him and not me? Finally, I tried to analyze it in a systematic way. I thought to myself, What could possibly happen in my life to bring me such a windfall? and bleakly I realized there was nothing. I had no old stock that would shoot up in value nor, as far as I was aware, did my family. I had no land where someone might suddenly find oil; I had no paintings that might turn out to be old masters;

I had no talents that someone was going to miraculously discover overnight to make me famous—I had nothing going for me.

And right there in the dormitory bed I said to myself, "Charlie, if you want something like that to happen in your life, you've got to plant some seeds, and you'd better plant a lot of them, cause you can't tell which ones will sprout."

Since then I have always been a planter of seeds. A few of them have sprouted, and there I am.[4]

To move forward successfully in life, we must have direction—and like the story says, "Plant seeds."

"Where Are You Going?"

When I married Kathy, back in 1980, I knew I would be taking on extra responsibility to support not only my new wife, but to finish graduate school. So I was thankful for my job driving for the city transit company in my big city.

My job gave me lots of time for people watching. I was always amazed at those who aimlessly wandered the sidewalks of downtown, looking as if they weren't sure where they were going.

It was even more interesting to watch some of them running for my bus as I pulled into a service stop. They would run without knowing what bus line they were chasing. There was no planning on their part, just chasing and hopping on a stopped bus.

Some of the runners would ask me, "Where are you going?"

I would immediately return their question by asking, "Where are you trying to get to?"

The answer was often the same, "Well, I'm not sure!"

On one particular afternoon, I had just pulled into a service

---

[4] David Campbell, *If You Don't Know Where You Are Going, You'll Probably End Up Somewhere Else* (Grand Rapids, MI: Niles Communications, 1974) 28–30.

stop when a senior lady came running up to board my bus all out of breath. She boarded and took a seat five rows back on the right side.

She rode the entire bus route, some fifteen miles out of the city. Upon arriving at the end of the line, everyone got off the bus except for this little lady.

As I turned off my engine, she curiously asked, "Are we in Forest Grove, Oregon?"

I chuckled and answered, "No, ma'am! This is the number 5 bus line."

She sounded so troubled when she replied, "Oh dear!"

She should have caught the number 57 downtown that stopped directly behind my bus. However, she was so distracted in running to catch the bus, she read the number 5 as 57 (a mistake many people made—especially those who run for buses).

Then she said, "I have a doctor's appointment at 2:00 p.m. Now what do I do?"

As I looked at my watch, I saw it was already 1:50 p.m. Even if she boarded a helicopter, there was no way she was going to make her appointment that afternoon since she was well over forty miles away—in the wrong direction.

Being directionless can be frustrating. No wonder GPS systems are now standard in new cars, as well as in cell phones.

Have you heard about a WW II ghost bomber known as the "Lady Be Good"? This B-24 was lost for some sixteen years until it was discovered by an oil exploration team.

The B-24 was headed for a bombing mission near Naples, Italy, some 1,800 miles away. Because of poor visibility or engine trouble, it was returning to Benghazi low on fuel.

But the plane and her nine man crew flew over 400 miles in the opposite direction from its target in the Libyan desert when it crashed. All nine crew members bailed out but all later perished in the desert where temperatures rose to 130 F. during daylight hours.

Life is filled with bumps and unexpected turns, sometimes detours. Being lost is a scary thing. Sometimes it takes those lost moments to capture our attention.

Again, and again, the Bible offers us a compass to help us through life.

Solomon said, "Trust in the LORD with all your heart, and do not lean on your own understanding. In all your ways acknowledge him, and he will make straight your paths" (Prov. 3:5–6 ESV).   Jeremiah reminds us, "Call to me and I will answer you and tell you great and wonderful things you do not know" (Jer. 33:3 HCSB).

Almighty God knows that we are like sheep and can easily be lost. In those intense moments when we are not sure which direction we should go, we can call upon the God of the universe to guide us.

D #3: Disjointed

Being disjointed means not making good sense in logic or behavior. It's the description of someone who is out of control like an airplane spiraling downward, heading for a crash.

Being disjointed is being caught up in a state of trouble— when circumstances move from bad to worse. This has a way of strangling our reasoning powers—placing them in the doghouse of uncertainty.

Just speak to anyone who has just gone through a nasty whirlwind which tears up everything in its path—the kind of whirlwind that destroys a marriage or family relationships.

Selfishness is often the culprit which can cause precarious storms to spring up out of nowhere, cause pain, remorse, and anxiety, and result in impotent, fragmented relationships.

> Now if your experience of Christ's encouragement
> and love means anything to you, if you have known

something of the fellowship of his Spirit, and all that it means in kindness and deep sympathy, do make my best hope for you come true! Live together in harmony, live together in love, as though you had only one mind and one spirit between you. Never act from motives of rivalry or personal vanity, but in humility think more of each other than you do of yourselves. None of you should think only of his own affairs, but should learn to see things from other people's point of view. (Phil. 2:1–4 Phillips)

D #4: Discouraged

Being discouraged is not a lot of fun. Everyone gets discouraged at one time or another. Even the apostle Paul, a servant-leader of God, became discouraged at one time in his ministry.

In 2 Corinthians 1:8 (NIV) he talks about the troubles he and his co-workers experienced in Asia. He said, "We were under great pressure, far beyond our ability to endure, so that we despaired of life itself."

In dealing with others, I am always quick to inform them that discouragement is only a temporary loss of perspective. With a little time and distance, the clouds will dissipate, and they can once again enjoy happy days.

At our church we have something called Grow Groups. This is a group of people from the church who come together for the purpose of sharing life and encouraging one another. It's a place where people can go for acceptance, support, and prayer.

What's amazing about these small groups, is if one of the members goes into the hospital, the group members become like family. They will step in not only visiting their sick member in the hospital but taking care of that member's family by bringing food to the home, and even helping with house chores until that member returns home.

I'm not sure how people think they can be lone rangers, trying to handle life alone. Doing life alone is especially hard for those who lack friends and family.

Small groups can be the answer to those "survivalists" who are lonely, trying to work out the kinks and hardships in their lives. If you need prayer or fellowship, or if you are looking for answers and hope, I would strongly encourage you to become part of a small group of believers. That would be a great decision for you this year.

We all need to be part of a community that can help encourage us in our times of great need. In 1 Corinthians 1:10–11 (NIV), the apostle Paul speaks again of this truth. "He has delivered us from such a deadly peril, and he will deliver us again. On him we have set our hope that he will continue to deliver us, as you help us by your prayers. Then many will give thanks on our behalf for the gracious favor granted us in answer to the prayers of many."

Chapter Eight Review
First Things First

Discussion:

To simplify life and get where you want to go, it is wise to make plans. Plans need to be thought through carefully to keep us out of those unpredictable zigzag heartbreaks.

1. List the four Ds in chapter 8.
2. What distracts you the most in life?
3. Why is putting first things first so important to success?
4. Knowing where you are going is a priority. Why?
5. What does it mean to be disjointed? Discuss.

Goal Setting

What are some goals you would like to achieve as you have read chapter eight?

_____

_____

_____

_____

_____

_____

CHAPTER NINE

Stay Focused

During my seminary days, I had a Greek professor who like clockwork would give an opening encouragement pitch each morning before class began. He would say, "If you are struggling to stay up to speed with the rest of the Greek scholars in learning Greek, then you need to get with the program!"

It must have worked, because all the guys in my class made it through this intense "Baby Greek" program by pursuing excellence, learning how to persevere, and exercising iron discipline in getting our assignments done and turned in on time.

After successfully completing this exhaustive nine-academic-hour program, I was surprised to learn from upper classmen that the Baby Greek program I had just finished was not the hardest course in the curriculum of this educational institution. I was informed that there were other courses like hermeneutics, apologetics, and New and Old Testament critical problems that were going to be as challenging.

Learning to stick with the program was the secret in not succumbing to those arduous classes that had a tendency to wear me out. All it took was applying that Greek principle "get with the program."

Stick with It

If you are stuck in a mindless job, or in a difficult marriage, and there seems to be no way out of your zigzag circumstances, let me be the first to encourage you. Do not quit! Just stick with the program.

I've told you about the job as a transit driver that I thought was going to be a dream job. Other seminary students driving for this transit company told me they had no problem driving and keeping up with their school schedules.

After six months, the job began to become burdensome. There seemed to be all kinds of hurdles in dealing with difficult people riding the public transit system to and from work.

The most annoying to me was dealing with fare evaders who refused to pay their bus fares. Others tried to sneak on open containers of food or alcohol beverages.

When trying to reason with some of these individuals to comply with company policy, it sometimes got nasty. Sometimes, this ended up as a verbal altercation that eventually led to a complaint against me.

The bus company was a toothless tiger that trained their drivers to look the other way to avoid those nasty complaints. They made it clear that their drivers were being paid big bucks to get along with the public.

The only problem with this fuzzy thinking was they forgot about their employee sitting in the hot seat taking all the verbal punches and jabs. Drivers sometimes were physically assaulted. To add insult to injury, the company treated them as if they were the problem.

"What did you do to create the problem?" a driver would be asked. Or, "What could you have done to have prevented this issue getting out of hand?" It was just assumed that the driver was the culprit.

One day my operator number was listed on the board when I checked in for duty. That meant my supervisor wanted to see me in his office. Normally this meant there was a complaint. After a brief visit, I learned there was indeed a complaint from the week prior.

After hearing for the umpteenth time what I could have done to have prevented this complaint, I had had it! I finally blurted out, "Yes, there is a way I could have averted that complaint."

My supervisor, eager to hear me spill my guts on the frivolous complaint said, "Continue on, Tom, so I can complete this form."

I chuckled and said, "I could have called in sick that day."

I felt the bus drivers were always put on the defensive while the customer was coddled and protected. After about a year, the honeymoon was over for me. From that point on, each morning became a drudgery as I dragged myself out of bed to go to a thankless job that I deeply resented.

It was only an eight block walk down to the bus company from where I lived. Instead of appreciating the birds singing and a gorgeous sunrise, I found myself walking each step praying, "Please, God, release me from this dreadful job."

Deep down inside I knew finding another job that paid as well, had good benefits, and gave me time to attend classes at the seminary was non-existent.

It seemed the more I prayed, the quieter God became. Over time, it was difficult to see fellow employees from the seminary hang up their steering wheels and leave driving bus for nice, cozy ministries while I was forgotten and left behind.

I tried everything to remain optimistic. When I wanted to quit, those words "get with the program" came back to haunt me. Looking into the rear-view mirror, I find it unbelievable that I spent twenty four laborious years working as a transit bus operator for this bus company.

It wasn't easy, but by the grace of God, He allowed me to use my time wisely. I made it a goal to study, and I graduated with a master of divinity degree, and a doctor of ministry degree while employed there. Aiming for those two degrees gave me peace of mind as I finished out those difficult years.

Then one day it happened. I had just officiated a funeral for one of our employees and had driven back to the company to turn the paperwork into the benefits department. As I was ready to step onto the elevator to head down to the main floor, I heard my name being called out. As I turned around, it was the benefit secretary who asked me to follow her back to her office.

Stepping into her office, she politely asked me to take a seat. She turned her computer screen around so I could read my name in bold black letters with my employment history on it.

Then she spoke these heavenly words, "Tom, you are eligible for retirement with full benefits on your upcoming birthday."

My mouth dropped, and for the first time, I was without words.

I asked if I could call Kathy from the office. I gave Kathy the news and she screamed with joy, saying, "Tom, retire!"

So, I did! At that point I realized God had not forgotten me. He sovereignly used all those testing moments to groom, shape, and prepare me for something special—something I would love and enjoy the rest of my life. Staying with the program was one of the best lessons I've learned in life.

When I wrote this chapter, I was in Kisumu, Kenya ministering to the most wonderful people on Planet Earth. I'm connected with the All Nations Pentecostal Evangelical Fellowship of Africa ministry (PEFA) there. It's obvious this special ministry was designed just for me. It fits me perfectly like a hand in a glove. I feel fortunate to have passed the test of time by sticking with the program to prepare me for this. These are my happiest moments, and I would not trade them for anything.

When the Call Didn't Come

Back in the late eighties, Kathy and I were involved at a local church in the Sellwood area of Portland, Oregon. I began working side by side with the elderly pastor who happened to be a professional counselor.

One day as we were riding to a ministry event, he casually mentioned he had taken note of some extraordinary abilities that he appreciated in me. As we were riding along, he made a point of telling me, "Don't be too quick in settling for just an ordinary pulpit."

As I looked at him with a question in my eyes, he added, "Expand your horizons. Think outside the box in ministering to people."

It wasn't my preaching skills he was noticing, but how I dealt with people in a positive way. He thought I could be more productive working with people being stuck behind a typical pulpit.

As we reached our destination, I was not in full agreement with his observations about my philosophy of ministry. In fact, I was appalled that he was taking the time to analyze me.

The more I thought about his words, the more offended I became. I had studied and trained at one of the best seminaries in the country. Neither he nor anyone else was going to talk me out of changing my course in ministry.

When I returned home that afternoon, I was determined to update my resume and to prove this pastor wrong. I even contacted the seminary placement department and asked them to send my resume out to the eleven western states, which they did.

I was determined to find a vacant pulpit in a Conservative Baptist Church. After several months of trying to locate one, responses to my resume fell silent. There simply were no churches looking for a pastor with my abilities and talents. It was awful!

A short time later, however, two churches popped up on the radar screen. I made contact but it became obvious after a series of exchanged phone calls that I was not the man they were looking for. Once again, my resume hadn't produced results. The whole thing was discouraging!

It wasn't until a couple years later I received a call from the Conservative Baptist Office, asking if I would be interested in pulpit supplying at one of their churches in the area. I was ecstatic and agreed!

After about three months of filling that pulpit, they called me as their senior pastor. I spent eight years at that church. One day it dawned on me that I wasn't all that thrilled and happy about my ministry there.

That is when I reflected on what the elderly pastor had told me. He knew what he was talking about. He was right! I felt stuck. My pulpit was indeed just an ordinary pulpit, and I felt it was holding me back from the things I really wanted to do.

Sunday after Sunday, it became more of a challenge to come into the pulpit enthused, with a smile on my face. That is when I decided to take a year's sabbatical to begin writing my first book, *The Whirlwind Principle*.

After leaving to write my book, a trucking company hired me part-time as a test pilot to test drive their new Freightliner trucks. I could easily write for a few days on my manuscript and then take a two-day break to go drive truck. It was a great schedule.

As my year was ending, and I was supposed to be heading back to my pulpit, I felt sluggish. Instead of looking forward to a grand reunion with my congregation, I lacked enthusiasm. That is when I decided it was time to resign and stay part-time with the trucking company up and until my book was finished.

Soon after the book was published, I was asked to drive full-time, and I accepted. It was a complete joy to spend the next year test driving new Freightliner trucks just off the factory line. This was a dream job. There's just something about that new truck smell. The company began flying me all over the United States to pick up a new truck or deliver a new truck across the country and fly back to Portland, Oregon. I simply loved this job! It was an opportunity to just to relax and enjoy these massive trucks.

One day I was assigned to deliver a bright, shiny, red Freightliner to San Jose, California. Upon delivering that new truck, I was informed there was a factory mistake. The truck was to be delivered to Des Moines, Iowa. My job was to get the truck to its appointed destination safely.

So I began heading across Interstate 40 making my way to New Mexico, then north to Iowa. On the way I went through the two churches that had shown some interest in calling me to be their senior pastor.

I could not believe what I was seeing. One of the locations was nothing more than acres of sand dunes and old buildings. It was an eyesore!

Miles later down the interstate was the second church that had showed interest in me. I made a point to stop and grab a quick bite to eat, and to look around. While finishing up a hamburger, a police officer came and sat directly in the booth in front of mine. Our eyes met and we struck up a friendly conversation.

He freely began telling me about his job and the community. I learned a great deal as he spoke about the high crime rate, the drug/alcohol problem in the area, and the high number of divorces in the community.

I had heard enough. I politely excused myself and thought as I walked away from that diner, *God really has a sense of humor.* Here were two churches that turned me down, and I thought I was the problem. For years I had wondered about those two churches, until God gave me a paid tour and allowed me to see firsthand the trouble my family and I would have experienced at either of those places. I could see that God was sovereignly looking out for my best interests.

I no longer questioned the sovereignty of God. As I drove

through those two small towns, it was obvious that neither of them was a right fit for my DNA. God simply knew what was best for me.

I called Kathy to tell her what I had uncovered about those ministries that turned us down. We chuckled together about how that wise pastor I had worked with some years prior was totally on target when he said, "Tom, why take just an ordinary pulpit?"

Finding the Right Fit

Several years later, a former professor in my doctoral program called from his cell phone from a 747 just leaving Spain and invited me to a luncheon in Portland, Oregon. I accepted his invitation only to learn that he wanted my abilities and talents for an upcoming crusade that was to be held in Nairobi, Kenya in just about eight weeks. I was invited to be a professor teaching an evangelism class at Manna Bible Institute as well as speaking at a crusade there before heading back to the States.

Deeply surprised at the invitation, I was totally ecstatic. My decision to go proved to be one of the best decisions I have ever made. The role fit me perfectly. I was wired and soldered for this strategic ministry.

I found training and equipping young Kenyan Christian men and women to become effective church leaders a perfect way to glorify God with my abilities and talents. My personality and philosophy of ministry was an awesome fit for this ministry role.

Sticking with the program seems to be a vital test that we must pass if God is to move us forward in ministry. When we choose to do things our own way, ignoring God and the advice of spiritually key people in our lives, that is when life becomes a struggle and a regret.

In Swahili they say, *ku wa makini*, meaning "Stay focused—don't be distracted."

My Greek professor was spot on when he said in a gentle voice, "Get with the program."

Just do it!

> You are my hiding place;
>   you will protect me from trouble
>   and surround me with songs of deliverance.
>
> I will instruct you and teach you in the way you
> should go;
>   I will counsel you with my loving eye on you. (Ps.
> 32:7–8 NIV)

Chapter Nine Review
Stay Focused

Discussion:

"Stick with the program" is a great motto to help us go through life's zigzags. Staying focused is necessary in sticking with the program.

1. How does sticking with the program develop character?
2. List a challenge you've encountered where you passed the test.
3. Why does a loving, sovereign God allow trouble in a believer's life?
4. Can you pinpoint a Scripture proving God is sovereignly in control?
5. Discuss God's deep love and protection for His children.

Goal Setting

What are some goals you would like to achieve as you have read chapter nine?

_____

_____

_____

_____

_____

CHAPTER TEN

A Sense of Humor

Getting through that intense "Baby Greek" program was certainly a challenge for me. Over the years I've been asked, "How did you do it? How do you account for your success in learning Greek?"

I have to admit, it was by learning to have a sense of humor. I had to learn how to laugh and not take myself so seriously in order to move ahead and pass that course.

The ability to laugh at oneself, especially when life gets a little bumpy, is so necessary. Humor is that special ingredient that brings the best out in us and causes our spirits to lift and our workday to lighten.

In fact, possessing a little humor may just be your ticket to better health. Here's the principle: God wants you and me to be happy and flexible. He wants us to be pliable, regardless of our circumstances, as we move through stressful moments in life.

Learning to let things go and to keep walking forward is a great start in learning how to develop a good sense of humor. All it takes is immersing one's self in laughter. Humor will get you through those rough moments of each day.

Several months ago, I saw a video clip on the Internet that clearly demonstrated this truth. It showed a middle-age man boarding a crowded subway car. Since there was only standing room, he leaned against a horizontal chrome bar as the doors closed behind him.

As the train pulled away from the platform, he reached into his black leather jacket for his electronic tablet and began to read it. Within a second he began to chuckle with a smirk on his face. His chuckling soon turned into a contagious laugh, which then turned into robust, uncontrollable, unending laughter.

The camera zoomed in on the faces of tired passengers worn out from a busy day's work. As they took notice of the laughing man, they begin smiling. Soon everyone in the entire subway car was laughing with him.

I don't think you could watch this clip without having a big smile on your face.

Most health professionals agree that laughter is the best medicine for healing.

Perhaps that is why I get a huge kick out watching comedy. You know, those nostalgic television programs like *The Andy Griffith Show*, portraying Don Knotts as the simpleton deputy sheriff in a little sleepy town called Mayberry. Everything about this small-town buffoon totally cracks me up. When I watch his quirky, irresistible behavior, it erases all the bad things that may have frustrated me on that particular day.

King Solomon in the Old Testament put it this way:

> There is a time for everything,
>   and a season for every activity under the heavens:
> a time to be born and a time to die,
>   a time to plant and a time to uproot,
>   a time to kill and a time to heal,
>   a time to tear down and a time to build,

a time to weep and a time to laugh,
a time to mourn and a time to dance,
a time to scatter stones and a time to gather them,
    a time to embrace and a time to refrain from
embracing,
    a time to search and a time to give up,
    a time to keep and a time to throw away,
    a time to tear and a time to mend,
    a time to be silent and a time to speak,
    a time to love and a time to hate,
    a time for war and a time for peace.
(Eccl. 3:1–8 NIV)

Did you notice the "time to laugh" is in there? Life can get a little out of whack at times, and events may rob us of our peace of mind and happiness. Let's face it! Life is filled with all kinds of surprises. We just need to relax more and learn not to take life so seriously when things tend to get out of hand.

The best recipe for staying on top of things is to learn to step back and take a deep breath before reacting to those annoying irritants that have a way in grinding our gears.

Missing the Train

In 2019, Kathy and I experienced one of those unpleasant moments in Nairobi, Kenya. We were scheduled to leave for Mombasa on the express train and were to be at the train station a whole hour before it was to leave.

The storm began brewing when our Uber driver failed to show up. By the time another vehicle was called and hired, we only had thirty minutes to make the twenty five kilometer drive to the train station.

The clouds thickened when we learned that our driver was not connected with Uber. He was a new driver who had only had his driver's license for a few short months. That became quickly evident when he did not know how to maneuver around all the heavy traffic and construction.

The driver had to make a half a dozen stops asking directions to the train station. We realized there was no way we were going to make the train. When we finally arrived at the station's main gate, a guard informed us the train had already left.

Since we were near the airport, we headed that direction. Our host, who was sitting in the front seat of the hired car, made a call and discovered that flying to Mombasa was going to cost us more than $600 in US funds for the flight. The only other choice at that point was to take a bus.

As our hired driver maneuvered his car back toward the city of Nairobi, he picked up his cell phone to make a call, got distracted, and he sideswiped another car. Now we were forced to sit in a hot car with no air-conditioning for an hour while our driver tried to settle with the other driver, along with a policeman who had witnessed the entire accident.

That is when Kathy and I started laughing at the whole situation. Only in Nairobi, Africa could this happen to us! Eventually, we made it to the bus station where we bought tickets and checked in our bags. What should have only taken four hours by train, took more than eleven hours riding on a bus all night to get to Mombasa.

Once we were on the bus and settled in, Kathy and I began reminiscing about the exasperating car trip with this inexperienced driver. We eventually broke out in a big laugh that made our whole day.

We concluded that God was still in control, and He had ordered our steps that day. If anything, it was just a test, and we needed to be good troopers and pass that test.

"And we know that in all things God works for the good of those who love him, who have been called according to his purpose"

(Rom. 8:28 NIV).

Here's the bottom line. Sometimes, we just need to stop taking things so personally. Getting upset and blaming others is not the answer. I can speak to that with some experience.

Putting Our Mistakes into Perspective

Since 1970, I've been a professional truck driver and bus operator, earning a twenty-seven-year driving award with the Smith System of Driving. After retiring from the city transit company, I returned to trucking, hauling everything from steel and lumber to freight.

At a small trucking company where I was hauling steel and lumber, the buildings sat on a very small piece of land. In fact, it shared its property with another company of mechanics who worked on cars and pickups.

That small piece of land is where our trucking company parked its seventeen trucks with their fifty-three-foot flatbed trailers. It was a very tight squeeze for us to maneuver around one another.

I had only been employed there for a short time when I managed to back into our workshop, creating a hole big enough for someone to walk through. Even though it was 2:00 a.m., and there were no outdoor lights, I should have been more careful.

If that wasn't embarrassing enough, about a year later I managed to sideswipe a parked car that was to be worked on by our neighbor mechanic. This was in broad daylight with everyone standing around watching me.

I must admit, I didn't feel like a very safe driver at that point (twenty-seven-year-award recipient or not). My self-esteem was at a low point. It wasn't until I left the company about a week later to go to Kenya, Africa as a conference speaker that things began to settle down for me.

Being gone for six weeks gave me the golden opportunity to

rethink that whole driving scenario. I came to realize that not everything is perfect in life. In fact, if you listen to traffic reports (regardless where you live), you'll hear many accident reports each day. That helped me in putting my own situation into perspective.

It's like the elderly grandmother who accidentally smashed her car into a train as it crossed in front of her. The train engineer was so upset that he climbed off his engine and began yelling, "What's the matter with you? Are you blind?" Her response was profoundly funny as she replied, "I hit you, didn't I?"

Proverbs 17:22 (NIV) says, "A cheerful heart is good medicine, but a crushed spirit dries up the bones."

In *Growing Strong in the Seasons of Life*, pastor and author Charles Swindoll wrote:

> Honestly now . . . how's your sense of humor? Are the times in which we live beginning to tell on you—your attitude, your face, your outlook? If you aren't sure, those who live under your roof, they'll tell you!
>
> Solomon talks straight, too. He (under the Holy Spirit's direction) says that three things will occur in the lives of those who have lost their capacity to enjoy life:
>
> 1. A broken spirit,
> 2. A lack of inner healing, and
> 3. Dried-up bones.
>
> What a barren portrait of the believer![5]

The good news is that people do not have to choose to live with a broken spirit or dried-up bones. Life is hard enough. There are some things we can do to cultivate a good sense of humor:

1. Hang out with cheerful people.

---

[5] Charles R. Swindoll, *Growing Strong in the Seasons of Life* (Colorado Springs: Multnomah Press, 1977), 103.

2. Learn to laugh more. People love happy people.
3. Smile. Practice kind, thoughtful words to say.
4. Read the cartoon/comic section in *Reader's Digest*.
5. Use every opportunity to encourage others.

"This is the day the Lord has made. Let us rejoice and be glad today" (Ps. 118:24 NLT).

Regardless of what others have done to you, learning to forgive, and moving on with a sense of humor will make you feel like a new person. It will free you from ill will and feelings of hatred, and it will give you a better outlook on life, putting a song in your heart.

The apostle Paul gives us some great counsel in these words of hope: "But I do concentrate on this: I leave the past behind and with hands outstretched to whatever lies ahead I go straight for the goal—my reward the honour of being called by God in Christ" (Phil. 3:12–14 Phillips).

Chapter Ten Review
A Sense of Humor

Discussion

Believers can learn to laugh at themselves, especially when zigzag moments catch them off guard. Having a sense of humor relaxes our minds as we learn not to take ourselves so seriously.

1. Having a sense of humor is a choice. Agree/disagree?
2. Why is laughter the best medicine during the hard times in life?
3. Do you agree with Solomon's counsel in Ecclesiastes 3:1–8 that there is a time for everything?
4. Do you believe God actually works all things out for good? (Read Rom. 8:28.)
5. Give a testimony how God worked out a zigzag for you.

Goal Setting

What are some goals you would like to achieve as you have read chapter ten?

CHAPTER ELEVEN

The Big Picture

I have to tell you about the day when I woke up sick and grumpy. I had no business in showing up at the bus company that morning to drive my designated bus route.

I had not been sleeping much as I was juggling school projects, papers and my driving schedules. Especially during midterms and final exams, everything became a little crazy, resulting in mood swings on my part. Since I didn't have the luxury calling in sick, I dragged myself down to the bus company to fulfill my obligation.

That particular morning, as I pulled into a service stop to board several passengers, I happened to notice a young man in his mid-twenties who appeared to be lackadaisically leaning against a building wall just several feet from the front door of my bus.

Since my bus schedule was down a couple of minutes, I yelled at him to hurry up and board. My voice must have growled when summoning him to board, since I drew attention from all my passengers starring at him.

That is when he bent down to grab two crutches to balance his walk as he made his way to my front door. It became evident that he had a serious walking condition and could not walk without those crutches. Sick or not, I felt so embarrassed and out of line with my attitude.

There's a Swahili word used when someone has really goofed up big time. It's *magenga*, pronounced (ma-gee-ga). It simply means "idiot."

That whole experience shook my self-centered little world that morning. You see, I didn't have the big picture when it came to taking care of the needs of others. I was too caught up with myself.

Global Positioning Needed

I needed a global positioning system (GPS) to give me the big picture so the whole scenario could have been avoided.

Wouldn't it be nice to have a system where we could get the big picture to see around corners, through walls, or even see miles way ahead of us like Jesus could do. It would certainly cut down on much of our frustrating moments in life.

Unfortunately, on this side of glory, we are stuck with earthly boundaries. There's no escaping time, distance, or space. We are fleshly, finite people, trapped in human bodies and limited in what we can and cannot do.

Not so with almighty God. He is infinite and not affected by our human limitations. To say He is infinite means He stepped into time without surrendering His eternality. That means He authored time and is not affected by it.

As human beings we have a past, present, and future. But in God's existence, there is no such division.

Professor Robert Cook pointed out in my seminary theology class, "God is the 'I am.' To Him, past, present, and future are one 'eternal now.' This does not mean that time has no objective reality to God. He recognizes the distinctions between past, present, and future, but He sees the past and future as vividly as He does the present."[6]

Scripture affirms this. "At just the right time Christ will be revealed from heaven by the blessed and only almighty God, the King of all kings and Lord of all lords. He alone can never die, and he lives in light so brilliant that no human can approach Him. No human eye has ever seen him, nor ever will. All honor and power to Him forever! Amen" (1 Tim. 6:15–16 NLT).

Henry Thiessen clearly describes God as being self-existent. That means that all finite space is dependent upon Him. Thiessen writes:

> God is also infinite in relation to time. He is without beginning or end, He is free from all succession of time, and He is the cause of time. That He is without beginning or end may be inferred from the doctrine of His self-existence; He who exists by reason of His nature rather than His volition, must always have existed and must continue to exist forever.[7]

Years ago I could have saved myself a lot of trouble and grief if I could have only seen the big picture for my future. I spent a lot of time chasing the wrong things, as well as making some really dumb mistakes along the way.

That bus job was one of the biggest headaches in my life. I spent twenty-four years dragging myself down to that company, even in sickness, chasing the carrot of money. I had a lack of interest in what I was doing in that job. All I could think about was my lack of purpose as I did the same old thing day after day. It was simply meaningless to me. I felt like a squirrel running on a spinning wheel inside an empty cage. I was running endlessly, going nowhere.

---

[6] Robert W. Cook, "God, Man, Christ" class notes, Western Seminary, Portland, OR, 1982, 159.

[7] Henry C. Thiessen, *Lectures in Systematic Theology* (Grand Rapids, MI: Wm. B. Eerdmans Pub. Co., 1981), 76.

Here's how Solomon, King David's son, described meaning in life.

> "Everything is meaningless," says the Teacher, "completely meaningless!"
>
> What do people get for all their hard work under the sun? Generations come and generations go, but the earth never changes. The sun rises and the sun sets, then hurries around to rise again. The wind blows south, and then turns north. Around and around it goes, blowing in circles. Rivers run into the sea, but the sea is never full. Then the water returns again to the rivers and flows out again to the sea. Everything is wearisome beyond description. No matter how much we see, we are never satisfied. No matter how much we hear, we are not content.
>
> History merely repeats itself. It has all been done before. Nothing under the sun is truly new. Sometimes people say, "Here is something new!" But actually it is old; nothing is ever truly new. (Eccl. 1:2–10 NLT)

My problem was that I lacked interest in what I was doing for a job. I wasn't thinking about the big picture. I did not have an overview of what was completely involved in driving the public to and from work. All I could think about was money—getting a paycheck!

I missed the fact that this job was giving me a strategic opportunity to finish seminary and providing a way to continue my studies in obtaining a doctor of ministry degree, and helping me move forward in life.

There is another big piece to the puzzle I also missed while working for this company. It gave me the opportunity to learn how to get along with the public. And sticking with it allowed me to collect a healthy retirement. I didn't see this truth until I actually retired in 2006. I found it unbelievable that they would provide me a monthly paycheck for the rest of my life, not to mention fully paid medical benefits that anyone would enjoy having. Totally unbelievable!

The bottom line is simple here: Do not be resentful about your life without looking at the big picture. Don't miss out on what God has graciously given you and your family. Do you remember the old gospel song "Count Your Blessings"? Written by Johnson Oatman Jr. back in 1897, its words can provide some contemporary guidance for us as we strive for faithfulness in serving Christ our Lord—wherever He has led us.

Count Your Blessings

When upon life's billows you are tempest tossed
When you are discouraged, thinking all is lost
Count your many blessings name them one by one
And it will surprise you what the Lord hath done

Count your blessings, name them one by one
Count your blessings, see what God hath done
Count your blessings, name them one by one
And it will surprise you what the Lord hath done

Are you ever burdened with a load of care?
Does the cross seem heavy you are called to bear?
Count your many blessings, every doubt will fly
And you will be singing as thew days go by

Count your blessings, name them one by one
Count your blessings, see what God hath done
Count your blessings, name them one by one
And it will surprise you what the Lord hath done

When you look at others with their lands and gold
Think that Christ h s promised you His wealth untold
County your many blessings, money cannot buy
Your reward in heaven, nor your Lord on high

Count your blessings, name them one by one
Count your blessings, see what God hath done
Count your blessings, name them one by one
And it will surprise you what the Lord hath done

So amid the conflict, whether great or small
Do not be discouraged, God is over all
Count your many blessings, angels will attend
Help and comfort give you to your journey's end

Count your blessings, name them one by one
Count your blessings, see what God hath done
Count your blessings, name them one by one
And it will surprise you what the Lord hath done

Sometimes we have to look at the big picture to enjoy what we have in life.

God's plans for us are good. He says, "I know what I'm doing. I have it all planned out—plans to take care of you, not abandon you, plans to give you the future you hope for" (Jer. 29:11 MSG).

Chapter Eleven Review
The Big Picture

Discussion:

If we don't see the big picture, we won't have enough information to draw proper conclusions. A lot of lessons are learned the hard way, just as I encountered while driving bus. We can avoid trouble and grief by considering the big picture, and trusting God for our times, and our futures.

1. Why is getting the big picture so important?
2. Short-circuit thinking will always lead to trouble. Why?
3. Learning the big picture starts at home. Agree or disagree?
4. Solomon in Ecclesiastes 1:1–10 says, "Everything is meaningless." What do you think he meant?
5. Have you been misunderstood? Share how God has used this for your good.

Goal Setting

What are some goals you would like to achieve as you have read chapter eleven?

CHAPTER TWELVE

Stay on Track

Failure to apply levelheaded thinking leads to unwise decisions and poor choices.

If you talk to those who have gone to prison, or who have been locked up in jail, they will acknowledge their wrong thinking robbed them from experiencing a happy and productive life.

Just before I retired from the transit district in Portland, Oregon back in 2006, I drove for a transit company that had a special bus route transporting some of these folks I'm writing about.

On that route a cool-looking guy about six feet tall with naturally curly brown hair climbed aboard my bus. I could tell he was sizing me up and watching my every move as I drove him to his workplace every morning.

After we had developed a relationship of trust, he began telling me about his checkered past. In a serious voice, he lowered his head in shame as he told me he had been released from prison about a year earlier. Then he told me this story.

One afternoon he was feeling just plain tired of life. On his way home he walked by a bank. The thought popped into his mind, *I should just walk in and rob it.* That's exactly what he did.

The next day the police showed up at his home and arrested him in front of his family. He was escorted to jail and was later convicted of first degree bank robbery.

Each morning as he rode my bus to work, he would continue his story about how his senseless thinking cost him his family, home, and job—the whole works! Now he was riding a bus going to a job that had high expectations of him. The job expected him to show up each day, clean shaven, and on time.

"How are you able to keep focused?" I asked.

"I'm just grateful to be out of the prison system, to be free without someone standing over me blowing a whistle, telling me what to do."

Just speak to anyone going through a divorce, or someone who's in the middle of a court battle, and you'll find out getting stuck in the legal system is not a fun experience. It's not only expensive, it's time consuming as the wheels of justice move very slowly. The legal system is not designed to be friendly. In fact, it's designed to be impersonal and embarrassing. Its purpose is to discourage people from getting caught up in its ugly web.

Keeping life simple means we need to take responsibility for our actions, and stay clear of obstacles that can entangle and cause regret. It also means keeping one's composure under control until the right moment to work it out between those involved.

Remember, "But the fruit of the Spirit is love, joy, peace, forbearance, kindness, goodness, faithfulness, gentleness and self-control. Against such things there is no law" (Gal. 5:22 NIV).

Handling Difficult People

God had a plan for the children of Israel that involved saving them from experiencing grief and possible death, but the exiled people had different ideas. They wanted to do things their own way. Sound familiar?

The Frank Sinatra syndrome of "I'll do it my way," is still alive and well today. People will do what they choose to do and what pleases them. The apostle Paul in the New Testament describes this kind of behavior as toxic when he penned the following words:

> But mark this: There will be terrible times in the last days. People will be lovers of themselves, lovers of money, boastful, proud, abusive, disobedient to their parents, ungrateful, unholy, without love, unforgiving, slanderous, without self-control, brutal, not lovers of the good, treacherous, rash, conceited, lovers of pleasure rather than lovers of God. (2 Tim. 3:1–4 NIV)

I facilitated a "Theories of Counseling" course at African Nazarene University in Kenya where I taught my students how to handle these kinds of difficult people.

After completing that counseling course, I redeveloped my personal counseling approach in dealing with toxic people. I advised my clients to simply back away when feeling threatened by angry people, whether at church, in the workplace, or at holiday dinners.

Some folks have the tendency to take over control of a conversation, and not listen to others. They try to abuse by using their power. Gary Thomas, in his book *When to Walk Away*, points out a vital principle when it comes to people who clearly disrespect the rights of others. He writes, "Controlling behavior is toxic behavior."[8]

---

[8] Gary Thomas, *When to Walk Away* (Grand Rapids, MI: Zondervan, 2019),

Here's the best counsel I can give anyone in these kinds of testy circumstances. You have a choice in moments when someone tries to bully, overpower, belittle, or manipulate you. Politely excuse yourself and to get out of there. Flee and don't look back.

Gary Thomas points out the crowd was upset with Jesus. They didn't like Him or His message. They were willing to do anything to get rid of this religious leader—even going so far as to try to throw Him off of a cliff. In Luke 4:30 (NCV) it says, "But Jesus walked through the crowd and went on his way." He handled a toxic situation where people were trying to destroy Him and His message by walking away.

Keep it Simple

Can I tell you what really grinds my gears? It's when I go into a store to buy a wagon or bicycle for one of my grandkids, only to have it brought out to me in a huge box. I then have to figure out how everything fits together. What's even more disturbing are all the little baggies filled with weird-looking screws, nuts, and bolts that fall out of the box.

It's like I have to be an engineer to assemble this thing. There may be a possibility that I lack an aptitude for reading and following ambiguous directions with their funny little pictures and an abundance of arrows pointing everywhere. God simply didn't wire and solder me that way. My DNA is different.

Perhaps the acronym KISS—"Keep it Simple Sam" is something companies that make toys and bikes need to bear in mind.

Sometimes we make things too complicated and difficult—like trying to follow those printed directions that confuse even adults—especially people like me.

Keeping it simple takes all the zigzags out of it, making life more fun, palatable, and easy to manage. A word to the wise: Just keep it simple!

40.

"But I am afraid that, as the serpent deceived Eve by his craftiness, your minds will be led astray from the simplicity and purity of devotion to Christ" (2 Cor. 11:3 NASB).

GPS Troubles

Another gear grinder for me is using GPS which takes the place of road maps. GPS is a great tool that enables us to get where we are going without any confusion. It works fine most of the time, especially out on open roads, and in small cities. It's those other times, mostly in busy metropolitan cities, it can lead you on a wild goose chase, and get you into impossible predicaments.

On one of my trucking assignments, I was dispatched to fly to Detroit where I was to facilitate a shakedown of a new Freightliner that had just came off the assembly line.

The buyer was anxiously waiting to put this truck into service, so I was instructed to shake it down for just two weeks. Once it passed the tests, I was to deliver this truck to a company in Chicago, Illinois. Everything went like clockwork, and it passed without a problem. The next afternoon I left for Chicago to deliver that truck.

As I approached the toll booths outside of Chicago, I couldn't believe the many roads and highways that went in different directions. I was totally lost, and the traffic was horrendous. I didn't see anywhere I could safely pull over to park and get directions. So I found myself struggling to get through old town Chicago.

Finally I pulled up at a stoplight and asked a man on the street where the particular suburb I was looking for was located.

He yelled up at me, saying, "Go straight for nine miles and look to your left."

Grateful for that little piece of information, I followed his directions and within forty-five minutes I had found the trucking company.

After I flew back to Portland, the very first thing I did was go to a Best Buy store and purchase my very first GPS. Good thing, for not more than a couple days later, I was assigned to deliver another new truck to Chicago. My new GPS took me right to the location without a problem. Buying a new GPS was a simple solution to my problem. It has saved a lot of time and worry. I'm not sure what took me so long to invest in one.

The Blessing of Zigzags

While we welcome the straight paths in life, most of our life circumstances turn out to be a series of zigzags. Let's be real. Zigzags just are. There's no way around them. You can expect them to show up unannounced when you least expect them.

The biblical accounts of the lives of many—from Jacob to Joseph and many others—read like a rollercoaster of zigzags.

As a chaplain, I found all my cases were zigzag cases, otherwise my clients wouldn't need my counsel or help.

Don't let zigzags surprise or distract you as they are really blessings in disguise. If you are wise, you will allow them to do their best work by helping you to slow down to avoid making bad decisions. Welcome zigzags as a trusted friend—they may save you from having major regrets.

Those sharp angles, twists and turns slow us down, and help us to take another look at the roads we are traveling. In other words, it's those uncomfortable, irritating zigzags that keeps us out of trouble—and get us back on the straight and narrow.

Zigzags can be a breath of fresh air. They often provide a second opportunity in life, giving us time to rethink an impetuous decision that may be costly. Bad decisions can become a thorn in our flesh, and in some cases may haunt us over the next forty years.

Matthew 11:15 in *The Message* asks, "Are you listening? Really listening?"

Tragedy at Sea

We can learn a lesson about the importance of zigzags in the true account of the USS Indianapolis that experienced the worst sea disaster ever recorded in naval history.

This catastrophe took place three-quarters of a century ago. At its heart is a failure to see the importance of zigzags.

On July 30, 1945, during World War II, the USS Indianapolis, the United States Navy's heavy cruiser was sunk in the Philippine Sea after taking a couple torpedo hits from a Japanese submarine.

Just four days earlier, she had carried a big wooden crate from San Francisco, California all the way to island of Tinian where it was unloaded. The contents of the crate were top secret. No one, including the captain of the USS Indianapolis knew its contents.

Later, the world learned it was carrying the atomic bomb.

(I stood on that ghostly runway on the same island in 1968 that the B-29 took off from carrying the atomic bomb to Japan that fateful day. For me, it was indeed a memorable moment.)

Several days later, the Indianapolis and its crew were making their way from Guam. All the ships were ordered to sail on a straight course during daylight hours. At night they were ordered to zigzag.

Captain Charles McVay was told there were no Japanese submarines in the area, so he didn't request an escort. Without enemy subs in the area, he felt it was safe to sail in a straight course. He didn't follow the order to zigzag that all ships were to follow, especially at night.

There were something like a thousand ships in the ocean then, sending messages each day to give their status as they pulled into or exited ports. This became overwhelming and the navy command changed their procedure to help cut back on the chaos. Ships were informed they would not have to send a message if they were arriving or departing on schedule.

Somehow, the USS Indianapolis did not arrive on time. In

fact, someone had taken its name off the board, and no one had reported it. The sobering truth was, no one even knew the USS Indianapolis was missing.

On the fourth day, out on the Philippine Sea, the USS Indianapolis was torpedoed and destroyed.

Once the order was given to abandon ship, Navy and Marine men hit the shark-infested Pacific Ocean some 600 miles from the nearest land. They floated for about four days before being spotted by a military pilot making his way back to his airbase.

The book *Indianapolis*, a New York Times Best Seller by Lynn Vincent and Sara Vladic, records the details of the disaster. "Four days later, just after midnight, a Japanese submarine spotted Indy and struck her with two torpedoes. Three hundred men went down with the ship. As Indi sank into the yawning underwater canyons of the Philippine Sea, nearly nine hundred men made it into the water alive. Only 316 survived."[9]

The Navy put the blame on the captain, saying if the USS Indianapolis had had an escort, this travesty would have never happened. Captain McVay was court-martialed on two counts: failure to give the order to abandon ship, and failure to take preventive measures. Cleared of the first charge, he was found guilty of the second.

The emotional pressure put on the captain was severe. Besides the court-martial, he had to live with the pain of knowing hundreds of his men were eaten alive by sharks, or drowned after floating for four days in a shark-infested ocean.

In this tragic incident at sea, the consequences of not following through in taking zigzags were severe.

In geometry, the shortest distance between two points is indeed a straight line. That principle will never change. But in real life, zigzags can be for our own benefit.

---

[9] Lynn Vincent and Sara Vladic, *Indianapolis* (New York City: Simon and Schuster, 2018), 2.

If you choose to allow God to shape and grow you in the zigzags of life, you will be a blessed person. It's an exciting adventure to have God lead us in our lives. As believers we should be grateful for almighty God's protection.

Be open to the important lessons God will teach you along your journey. Walk in faith, relying on God's *good* intentions for your life, and accept those zigzags as friends and not as opponents.

Be strong and brave. Be sure to obey all the teachings my servant Moses gave you. If you follow them exactly, you will be successful in everything you do. Always remember what is written in the Book of the Teachings. Study it day and night to be sure to obey everything that is written there. If you do this, you will be wise and successful in everything. Remember that I commanded you to be strong and brave. Don't be afraid, because the LORD your God will be with you everywhere you go." (Josh. 1:7–9 NCV)

Chapter Twelve Review
Stay on Track

Discussion:

This chapter reminds the believer to keep things simple while walking the Christian pathway in life. Our omniscient God uses zigzags for our benefit, giving us the opportunity to steer clear of possible regrets.

1. Why is taking responsibility for our actions so important?
2. Why should believers walk away from toxic behavior?
3. Taking shortcuts in working out problems can be risky. Why?
4. What lessons can be learned from the USS Indianapolis tragedy?
5. Listening to the wrong voices may lead to unwanted problems. Explain.

Goal Setting

What are some goals you would like to achieve as you have read chapter twelve?

_____

_____

_____

_____

_____

Order Information

To order additional copies of this book, please visit
www.redemption-press.com.
Also available on Amazon.com and BarnesandNoble.com
or by calling toll-free 1-844-2REDEEM.

CPSIA information can be obtained
at www.ICGtesting.com
Printed in the USA
FSHW011733131221
86889FS